WESTERN OUTLAWS

WESTERN OUTLAWS
THE "GOOD BADMAN" IN FACT, FILM, AND FOLKLORE

Kent Ladd Steckmesser

Regina Books

Claremont, California

Library of Congress Cataloging in Publication Data
Steckmesser, Kent Ladd, 1928-
  Western outlaws.

  Bibliography: p. 147
  1. Outlaws – West (U.S.) – Biography.
  2. West (U.S.) – Biography.
  3. Outlaws in literature.
  4. West (U.S.) – History – 1848-1950. I. Title.
F594.S82   1983   364.1'55'9022 [B]   83-2854

ISBN 0-941690-07-5
ISBN 0-941690-08-3 (pbk)

Regina Books
Box 280 Claremont, CA 91711
Manufactured in the United States of America

CONTENTS

ILLUSTRATIONS

Preface

This book about outlaws of the American West is an introductory work, intended for the general reader and for students. It aims to provide basic information in a reliable and readable way, striking a balance between the scholarly and the more popular kind of work that seems to be predominant in this subject. Rather than a straight recital of the outlaws' misdeeds, it seeks to understand outlawry as a part of cultural history. The law-breakers were actual individuals, but some of them also became legendary or near-legendary figures in popular tradition. How and why they were accorded this role is something that the book tries to explain.

The standard against which many American outlaws have been measured is that of Robin Hood, the world's "classic" outlaw. Hence, we begin with a look at his legend for clues to recurrent themes that might be found in the American narratives. Then the careers of the more noted outlaws of the trans-Mississippi region are examined on a roughly chronological basis. The record of each individual's crimes is summarized, so far as it can be determined, from court files, newspaper reports, and other first-hand accounts. This biographical sketch is followed by an explanation of how the lawbreaker's popular reputation took shape in such media as folk songs and tales, novels, biographies, and motion pictures. In comparing these two sets of sources, it becomes evident that the folk imagination and commercial exploitation have reshaped history in accordance with a recurrent pattern of outlaw-idealization.

The outlaws chosen for inclusion here are those who achieved Robin Hood status over a period of time and in a variety of media. Jesse James and Billy the Kid head the list, with Joaquin Murrieta, Butch Cassidy, and Pretty Boy Floyd as other subjects. The criteria have led to the exclusion of several outlaws, such as the Daltons, because they never achieved the degree of legendary fame accorded the others. The favored ones came to be regarded as social idealists, who among other traits "took from the rich and gave to the poor." They also share personal traits missing in bad-badmen. They are, in legend if not in actuality, kind to children and poor widows, possessed of a sense of humor, and noted for their cleverness. They also embody extreme individualism, of a kind increasingly rare in our crowded world. So nostalgia is involved in our view of these riders of the wide open spaces.

Historians have always faced difficulties in trying to write about this subject. The reliability of the people who supply information about any criminal activity always has to be considered. The "inside" history of outlaw gangs is often based on the dubious testimony of ex-members who have turned state's evidence. Relatives of the outlaw, who may know the whole story, display clam-like responses to investigators' questions. More recently, denial of access to records because of federal and state privacy laws has been an obstacle to research. Then too, many writers romanticize the criminal's career. Whether this is done instinctively or purposely, the effect is to cloud the truth. But since the ability to distinguish fact from fantasy is essential to good citizenship and a happy life, a cool appraisal of the outlaws' significance must be undertaken.

Sources used in the text are identified in an annotated bibliography. This method has been chosen over conventional footnotes for purposes of brevity and readability. The section is also a review of some of the principal literature about the outlaws, so that those interested in pursuing the subject further may know how to go about it.

THE ROBIN HOOD LEGEND

Few people have ever thought of Robin Hood as a mean-tempered murderer and extortionist who ran a "protection racket" in Sherwood Forest. Instead, he's been viewed as a genial philanthropist who embodied the highest ideals of justice and sportsmanship. And where is it written that such an individual ever ranged the English woods?

Virtually all the information about this outlaw comes from folklore, specifically from fifteenth and sixteenth century ballads. The balladeers, in effect, created Robin Hood to please audiences who wanted to hear stories about a beneficent bandit. Four of these ballads were printed about 1500 under the title of *A Lytell Geste of Robyn Hode* (a "geste" being a tale of adventure), and this marks the beginning of a "biography." The ballads are all fuzzy in their historical details. They assign Hood to the reign of "Edward"; not too helpful, since three Edwards ruled in succession between 1272 and 1377. They say a little about the outlaw's social status, character, and exploits, but in a sketchy and generalized way. Yet the *Geste* is practically a textbook for outlaw biographies.

The first test of a "heroic" outlaw is that he fight for social justice. Robin Hood passes with flying colors, for he preys on nobles and churchmen who have grown fat while the commoners starve. The social situation underlying the ballads is that the established institutions have become corrupted to the point where injustice and oppression are the rule. The common people were subject to forest laws, which prescribed death for poaching, and they had to pay feudal dues and render services to the lords of the manor. The Church squeezed them by a system of tithes and other demands. The victims did not challenge the idea of a hierarchical society, nor did they resist the King, but they did attack individuals in the upper ranks who were considered to be unjust or corrupt. And the crimes of their champion, Robin Hood, were viewed as an effort to restore elementary justice.

So Robin Hood makes the higher clergy his target, instructing his men that "these bisshoppes and these archebishoppes/ye shall them bete and bynde." At the same time he remains devoted to the "pure" religion. He loves the Virgin Mother, and he prays three times a day. It is also noteworthy that in several encounters with the lower-echelon monks, he never robs those who are honest about the amount of money they're carrying. It appears that the bandit chief just can't stand liars and cheats.

The outlaw also robs the hated nobles. But here again there are "good" noblemen whom Robin Hood not only spares but even helps. Sir Richard of Lee is about to lose his estate because he cannot repay a loan to the grasping abbot of St. Mary's. Robin Hood, after hearing this sad story, lends Sir Richard the 400 pounds that enable him to save his lands. Then the outlaw holds up the Abbot's clerk (in later ballads the Abbot himself) and takes *800* pounds. In time this type of anecdote becomes almost indispensible in outlaw narratives. Jesse James is said to have performed the same "loan service" for a poor widow in Missouri, and then robbed the mortgage banker to double his money.

Robin Hood never picks on "good yeomen," perhaps because he is described in the *Geste* as being of yeoman status. Nor does he bother women; no rapist he! Indeed, for a criminal, he seems incredibly polite and good-natured. As the *Geste* says with unconscious irony: "So curteyse an outlawe as he was one/was never none founde."

The *Geste* also alludes to Robin Hood's concern for the weak and the poor. The last stanza concludes that "he was a good outlawe/ and dyde pore men moch god." This was just the seedling for an idea that was to grow until it became central to the whole legend: "he took from the rich and gave to the poor." No one in 1500 was under the illusion that Robin Hood had been running a one-man Community Chest. Nor does the *Geste* have him handing out loot to the poverty-stricken. But in time this particular concept became so well rooted that it is now practically synonymous with the name of Robin Hood.

Robin Hood's principal adversary is the Sheriff of Nottingham, symbol of the oppressive political system. The lawman is a nasty, evil-hearted fellow and a double-crosser to boot. In one episode the bandits capture him, force him to sleep on the ground in his underwear, and make him promise to help them in any way he can. But the Sheriff is determined to avenge this humiliation, promise or no. His chance comes when Robin Hood goes to Nottingham in disguise and wins an arrow-shooting contest. The Sheriff recognizes him and tries to capture the band, but the outlaws escape after a hard fight. Later in the forest there is another slam-bang encounter, and this time Robin Hood kills his old enemy. In a display of primitive ferocity characteristic of the medieval ballads, he cuts off the Sheriff's head.

Robin Hood's fellow outlaws are also introduced in the *Geste*. Little John, Will Scathlock (Scarlet), and Much the Miller's Son are all genial extroverts just like their leader. They adhere to a Mafia-like code of loyalty, exemplified by rescues and other feats of derring-do. The fact that they are called Merry Men tells us that they enjoy life in the greenwood. And why wouldn't they? It always seems to be springtime, with the sun shining, birds singing, and deer browsing in the shadows. In outlaw legendry, it's never winter.

Two characters known in the modern version of the legend, Friar Tuck and Maid Marian, do not appear in the *Geste*. They are not added to the cast for another hundred years.

The final stanzas of the *Geste* relate Robin Hood's meeting with King Edward, and also present a version of his death by treachery. The King goes to the forest in disguise, but after his identity is revealed at the outlaw camp, Robin Hood and the Merry Men swear loyalty to him. Robin Hood even serves at the court for a while, but the appeal of the old life is too strong, and he returns to the forest. Finally, he goes to receive medical aid from his cousin, who is prioress of the nunnery at Kirklees. But this worldly lady has conspired with her lover, Sir Roger of Doncaster, to betray Robin Hood. So while being "purged" he is permitted to bleed to death, not the last outlaw to be done in by a woman.

Thus the *Geste* establishes a pattern, one to which later claimants to Robin Hood status must conform. 1) Robin Hood goes to the woods not because of a selfish desire for plunder, or because he is a social misfit. Oh no! He goes rather because of his passion for justice at a time of great injustice. 2) He administers a kind of "practical socialism" by robbing the haves and (by implication) giving to the have-nots. 3) He's no mad-dog psychopath, but an attractive person, jolly and virtuous. 4) He is a trickster, able to outwit the Sheriff at every turn. 5) He can only be brought down by treachery. Such is the portrait of the archetypal "good outlaw" for hundreds of years to come.

After the *Geste*, Robin Hood's legend continued to unfold in folklore, formal history, and stage drama. Broadside-ballads were the main channel for folklore in the sixteenth and seventeenth centuries. Broadsides were printed on single sheets of cheap paper, and were hawked by street singers or sold at bookstalls. They covered a wide range of topics, but Robin Hood was a popular subject from the start. In 1520, for example, John Dorne was retailing a "Robyn Hode" broadside at his bookshop in Oxford.

In these narratives the emphasis shifts somewhat from social justice to single combats and trickster tales. Robin Hood tangles with a variety of antagonists, using fists, swords, and quarterstaffs. The outlaw chief is no superman, for he is often defeated in these jousts. But he always takes the loss with good humor, and usually invites the winner to join his band. Such is the case in *Robin Hood and Little John*, when the two meet on a narrow footbridge. Neither wishes to give way, so they fight with staffs "as if they had been threshing corn." "Little" John, who is seven feet tall, knocks Robin Hood into the stream, but the drenched loser invites him to join the Merry Men.

The broadsides also portray the outlaw as a trickster hero. The outlaw, in real life as in folklore, often has to practice trickery to survive. But if he is to become a folk hero he must be credited with exceptional cleverness. So Robin Hood is continually outwitting the Sheriff by various devices, usually a disguise of some sort. The best example would be *Robin Hood and the Potter*, which dates from about 1500. Robin Hood fights with the potter, loses, but then changes clothes with him. He goes to Nottingham, where the disguise is so successful that he sells pots to the Sheriff's wife. He leads the Sheriff to the forest on the promise of catching Robin Hood, but once there robs him and sends him back to town stripped of his clothes and money.

In *Robin Hood and the Golden Arrow* the outlaw again goes to town in disguise. He wins the prized arrow in an archery contest. Then on his way back to Sherwood Forest, he shoots an arrow into town, with an attached note informing the Sheriff that he had been there. The Sheriff "rav'd like one that's mad," and the world has chuckled at his discomfiture ever since.

One of the later broadsides (about 1600) departs from the usual "jolly Robin" portrayal. In *Robin Hood's Progress to Nottingham*, the young man is on his way to compete in an archery tournament. He meets a fifteen-man party of the King's foresters who ridicule the stripling for his pretensions as a bowman. They wager him that he cannot hit a deer grazing at a considerable distance. Robin Hood brings the animal down, but the foresters refuse to pay the bet and instead order him to be gone. Then there is the chilling picture of a near-psychopathic killer at work. Robin Hood "laughs and smiles" at the foresters insults, moves a short distance away, and then opens up on them with his deadly bow. He kills all fifteen, "splitting their heads in twain" with the bullet-like arrows. It is not the killings alone, but rather that murderous smile that is at variance with the legend. The idealized outlaw is supposed to go about killing with a heavy heart.

Historians and dramatists also contributed to the legend. John Major was a Scottish historian whose *History of Greater Britain* was published at Paris in 1521. Writing in Latin, he called the outlaw "Robertus Hudus." All of the by-now conventional elements of the legend, evidently borrowed from the *Geste* and some of the earliest broadsides, are incorporated into his brief sketch:

> About this time, it was, as I conceive, that there flourished those most famous robbers, Robert Hood, an Englishman, and Little John, who lay in wait in the woods, but spoiled of their goods only those that were wealthy. They took the life of no man, unless either he attacked them or offered resistance in defence of his property.... The feats of this Robert are told in song all over Britain. He would allow no woman to suffer injustice, nor would he spoil the poor, but rather enriched them from plunder taken from abbots. The robberies of this man I condemn, but of all robbers he was the humanest and the chief.

Major's "about this time" refers not to one of the Edwards but to the reign of Richard the Lion-Hearted (1189-1199). This dating further scrambled the Robin Hood chronology. Major's source may have been some lost ballad linking Richard and Robin Hood. But once Richard was introduced, his contemporary Prince John could also be brought into the story. So at the end of the century Elizabethan dramatists would set their Robin Hood plays in the Richard-and-John period, coincidentally making John the villain that he now is in the legend.

Richard Grafton in his *Abridgement of the Chronicles of England* (1572) was another historian who followed Major in assigning Robin Hood to the reign of Richard I. But he made a significant contribution to the legend in his own right by asserting that the outlaw was "descended of noble parentage." This assertion was seized upon by the court playwrights Anthony Munday and Henry Chettle and incorporated into their dramas *The Downfall of Robert Earl of Huntingdon* and *The Death of Robert Earl of Huntingdon* (both 1598). As the titles indicate, they promoted the yeoman of the ballads to an earl, presumably to please the aristocratic audiences for whom they were writing. Before long, dilettante historians were busy trying to confirm the outlaw's noble birth, but after a fruitless search they had to manufacture a family tree for him.

The story and characters in the Munday-Chettle plays are basically those of today's children's books and movie scripts. Among the familiar *dramatis personae* are King Richard, Prince John, Friar Tuck, and Maid Marian. It is now recognized that Friar Tuck and Maid Marian were "borrowed" from the May Games. In the sixteenth century, troupes of revellers celebrated the coming of spring by dressing up as legendary personages. In the Morris dance particularly, Robin Hood, Friar Tuck, and Maid Marian were all popular characters. Their association in these festivals was what brought them together in the post-1600 stages of the legend.

As of 1600, then, the major outlines of the legend had been drawn. Robin Hood's love affair with Marian, his "noble" parentage, his concern for the poor, had already become clichés. The refinement and polishing of these conventions continued over the next three hundred years. Repetition of the familiar story convinced many that it must have been based on a historical situation.

And so it came to pass that historians were asked to unearth more information about the real man behind the legend. The scholars sweated and strained, but eventually they found that there had been no actual Robin Hood.

Why couldn't they find him? One major problem, as Thomas Wright said in 1846, was that "the character and popular history of Robin Hood was formed upon the ballads, and not the ballads upon the person." Then how reliable are the ballads as historical sources? In the sixteenth century "a tale of Robin Hood" was a synonym for a fictional story.

Another difficulty is chronological placement. The ballads are vague and contradictory here. The *Lytell Geste* refers to "comely Edward," but which of the three Edwards was that? The faceless authority "tradition" places Robin Hood in the reign of Edward II (1307-1327), principally because the documented occurrences of outlawry in that period seem to match the ballad story. Also, the most popular of the flesh-and-blood candidates has been located in this reign.

Joseph Hunter was a learned scholar who nominated this candidate in 1852. In the Court Rolls for the Manor of Wakefield he found references to one Robert Hood, a tenant at the Manor. In 1322 the Earl of Lancaster led a revolt against Edward II, but he was crushed at the battle of Boroughbridge, and his followers had their lands confiscated. Hunter maintained that Hood was one of these rebels who went to the forests after the battle. He also found in the Household Expense Accounts that Edward had made in 1324 several payments to a court valet named Robert Hood. This squares with the *Geste*, which has Robin Hood making peace with the King and then accepting service at court.

Hunter's discovery of these documentary references created quite a stir in the nineteenth century. But his trial balloon began leaking air, and it gradually crumpled to earth. Critics pointed out that Robert Hood was a common name in the fourteenth century. There were in fact six Robert Hoods referred to in a period of less than forty years during the reign of the three Edwards!

Further, Hunter's evidence does not prove that the Wakefield tenant was ever outlawed; the assumption that he was is based on circumstantial evidence. And the picture of the bold bandit becoming an obscure flunky at court is too much of a deviation from the ballads. Despite these problems, the "Wakefield Robin Hood" remains a popular choice, and in the 1950s two books were published in support of his candidacy.

Other historians have found their Robin Hoods in the thirteenth century. In 1230, the Pipe Rolls during the reign of Henry III say "the Sheriff of Yorkshire owes 32 shillings and six pence in the matter of the chattels of Robert Hood, fugitive." Unhappily, there is not much more to go on than this brief reference. Another theory holds that Robin Hood was a supporter of Simon de Montfort, who led an uprising against the same King Henry in 1265. The earl was defeated, but some of his followers continued their resistance and were outlawed. The problem here lies in the conflict with the ballads, which emphasize loyalty to the sovereign. Robin Hood resists unjust laws, but not the person of the king.

Sometimes physical landmarks have been cited as evidence for the outlaw's actual existence. There are "Robin Hood" caves, rocks, and cairns scattered all over the countryside from London through Scotland. Various relics, such as his bow and arrow, his chair, and his slippers, were exhibited for travelers in Notthingham as late as the eighteenth century. But such remains are clearly a mirror image of the legend. *Every* outlaw of reputation has caves and rocks named after him.

It may be that one of the "Robert Hoods" found in history was the original outlaw. But if he was, he bears little resemblance to the Robin Hood that has come down in song and story. It appears our hero is a composite of a number of outlaws, an ideal figure who belongs to the world of "once upon a time" rather than to earth-bound fact.

The arguments in favor of Robin Hood's legendary character seem all the more convincing in view of the substantial evidence concerning outlaws who *preceded* him. Hereward (fl. 1170), Fulk Fitzwarin (fl. 1200), and Eustace the Monk (died 1217) were also "traditional" outlaws, celebrated in ballads and folktales. Unlike Robin Hood, however, they can all be identified by contemporary documents. People and places in the stories are verifiable.

Assuming that Robin Hood was legendary, the crucial question is why his legend flourished while those of Hereward and the others faded. The reason may be the more democratic nature of his appeal. Hereward and Fulk Fitzwarin were from the nobility, and they performed among the rich and well-born. Robin Hood, despite his later conversion to an aristocratic figure, was of the yeomanry and fought for the rights of "pore men." Since the poor and weak always outnumber the rich and strong, it is clear why this imaginary bandit became the hero of a great popular epic.

So Robin Hood seems to have been invented as the people's protector. It is a recurrent folk belief that whenever there is "injustice," an outlaw like Robin Hood will appear on the scene to help right the situation. And in the world at large, wherever there have been unstable social or economic conditions, a Robin Hood is quite likely to be created as a symbol of resistance and rectification.

ROBIN HOOD CROSSES THE ATLANTIC

The Robin Hood legend was exported to North America in the seventeenth and eighteenth centuries. Emigrants coming to the colonies brought over some of the old ballads as part of their cultural baggage. A handful of these ballads remained alive in oral tradition right into the twentieth century. But American folk singers inevitably began substituting native-born outlaws for Robin Hood. Then too the American Revolution severed some of the cultural bonds with England, and folk heroes like King Arthur and Robin Hood lost favor along with Lord North and George III.

Actually, children's books and motion pictures have been more important than folklore in keeping Robin Hood alive in the popular memory. The children's books basically retell the ballads, both the *Geste* and the broadsides, but with heavy editing. Robin Hood does not cut off the Sheriff's head, does not kill fifteen foresters on his way to Nottingham, and in some versions is not even betrayed by the prioress of Kirkless ("and Robin Hood lived in the greenwood for the rest of his days" says one). The tone in practically all of these books is light-hearted, giving the impression that the life of an outlaw must be jolly good fun.

The most influential work was Howard Pyle's *The Merry Adventures of Robin Hood of Great Renown.* First published in 1883, it has gone through numerous reprintings ever since, and has thus educated four generations of American children. Pyle places the hero in the reign of Richard the Lion Hearted, but he wisely tells his readers that the stories occur in a "land of Fancy." There is moderate revision of the ballads. The account of how Robin Hood becomes an outlaw, in the broadside of his *Progress to Nottingham,* is altered so that he kills only one forester instead of fifteen. And he does not grin as he sets about his bloody work; rather "his heart was sick within him." For all the editing, the book was a fair rendering of the legend. Pyle was an accomplished illustrator, and much of the book's success can be attributed to his skillful drawings of the various episodes.

Cinematic representations of the outlaw have been another powerful influence on children and adults alike. Douglas Fairbanks, Sr. starred in the first major *Robin Hood* in 1922. The film broke box office records all over the place; it ran for twenty-five weeks at Grauman's Egyptian Theatre in Hollywood. (Streetcar conductors on Hollywood Boulevard, instead of calling the regular stop at McCadden Place, would announce "all out for *Robin Hood!*") Fairbanks was the ideal actor to embody the legend, since he had a carefree style. He was also a skilled acrobat, and there were numerous action scenes where he ran around Nottingham Castle eluding the Sheriff's men.

The financial and critical success of Fairbanks' film made remakes inevitable. Warner Brothers took the plunge in 1938, using Errol Flynn as the hero in their Technicolor superproduction, *The Adventures of Robin Hood.* This also was a very good film, and has been regarded as one of Hollywood's classics. The script included a representative selection of the ancient legends, such as the golden arrow contest, with the Munday-Chettle plays being the framework. *Film Daily* in its review, April 29, 1938, said that "athletic Errol Flynn is an ideal choice for the role of the bold, fearless knight of Sherwood Forest, and fights for the oppressed and robs the rich to aid the poor." He is a Saxon, "Earl of Sherwood and Nottingham," who resists the brutal Normans. However, as he explains to Maid Marian, "It's injustice I hate, not the Normans."

Flynn was supported by an outstanding cast, which included Claude Rains as Prince John, Olivia de Haviland as Lady Marian, and Alan Hale (who had played the same role with Fairbanks sixteen years before) as Little John. The Fairbanks influence was revealed in the chase sequences and action scenes. And in the era of Franklin D. Roosevelt's New Deal, the theme of Robin Hood's feeding and clothing the poor was forcefully stated. In one scene Robin Hood shows Marian a group of lame and halt Saxons that the outlaws are caring for, giving the impression that he was running an early-day welfare agency.

Further efforts at filming the Robin Hood saga followed the Fairbanks-Flynn pattern. The most important of these was the television series *Adventures in Sherwood Forest,* starring Richard Greene. Produced in England beginning in 1955, the series has been run or rerun in England and America ever since. Thus it is probably the source from which the most recent generation of children have learned about the legendary outlaw. Yet, audiences have not been happy with revisionist versions. The 1976 film *Robin and Marian* starred Sean Connery in a grubby interpretation. Robin

King Richard confers knighthood on Robin Hood (Errol Flynn) in *Adventures of Robin Hood.* Courtesy Warner Bros.-Seven Arts.

Hood is balding fleshy, and fiftyish. He kicks his opponents in the groin and has lost his idealism. Maid Marian and the prioress of Kirkless are rolled into one character! Neither audiences nor critics seemed willing to accept this destruction of the legend; the review of the film in *Newsweek* (March 22, 1976) was entitled "Cockeyed Robin."

Yet no one need worry about the survivability of the legend. With a proven record of six hundred years or so, it seems in no danger of disappearing. But in the nineteenth century various American outlaw legends began to rival that of the archetype. The basic formula remained the same, but the names, events, and locales reflected the more familiar circumstances of American history.

There were few potential "American Robin Hoods" until the mid-century. There was plenty of crime, but much of it was committed by vicious gangs whom no one could fit into the Robin Hood tradition. All of the earlier American bandits seemed to lack some of the prerequisites for heroic status. An example would be Michael Martin (1795-1821), better known by his alias of "Captain Lightfoot."

Martin was a native of Ireland, where he began robbing stages in 1816. He came to America in 1819 after the roads became too dangerous for him. Landing in Salem, Massachusetts, he was a moderately successful highwayman in the New England area for some two years. He tried to go straight for a time, but he drank and he gambled, two dangerous habits for anyone attempting rehabilitation. Martin told with some pride of how he learned to cheat at a card game called "The Honest Quaker." The disguise-theme reappears, with Martin posing as a physician, a Quaker, a "gentleman" both during and after his holdups. Despite his cleverness, he was trapped by officers in 1821 and went to the gallows at Cambridge, Massachusetts.

In the confession, which he left behind, Martin attempts to portray himself as another Robin Hood. His Irish mentor, a "Captain Thunderbolt," taught him not only the techniques of highway robbery but also some Robin Hood-like precepts: "He would get as much as he could from the rich, but would never molest the poor." Martin claimed that he and Thunderbolt helped a poor man whose cattle and furniture were about to be taken for tithes. They lent him 40 pounds to pay the minister. They then held up the minister and the excise officer on the road. This was a hoary anecdote even in 1821, when Martin's confession was published.

Despite Martin's pretensions, there are no Massachusetts folktales that would support his claim to Robin Hood stature. His self-admitted "disposition to intemperance and riot," along with his "vindictive and ill-tempered" nature, disqualify him. Legend might have reworked Martin's character into more heroic dimensions,* but there was still lacking that background of social conflict necessary for the Robin Hood type to emerge. In the Massachusetts of 1820 there was no widespread mistrust of the legal machinery, nor the kind of struggle between the haves and have-nots that seems to be the matrix for Robin Hood legends. So Martin did not become a personification of social justice. In legend he remains what he was in life: a thoroughly unattractive hooligan.

---

*W.R. Burnett attempted to romanticize Martin in his 1954 novel, *Captain Lightfoot,* but the story ends with the outlaw's departure from Ireland.

Richard Greene as Robin Hood fights one of the Sheriff's men in *Adventures in Sherwood Forest.* Courtesy Official Films, Inc.

Somewhat more promising is Martin's contemporary, David Lewis of Carlisle, Pennsylvania. Folklore remembered "Lewis the Robber" with some fondness, since he supposedly victimized only sheriffs and wealthy men. Lewis's father died when he was a young boy, a familiar feature in outlaw biographies. David then followed the wayward path, becoming an army deserter, counterfeiter, and jail escape artist. His principal hideout was at Doubling Gap Cave in Cumberland County, although there are a number of other Lewis's Rocks and Caves scattered through central Pennsylvania. After a series of robberies around Carlisle, Lewis was wounded in a gun battle and captured. He died in jail of gangrene on July 13, 1820, after dictating a confession.

Lewis's statement reveals him to have been much closer to the Robin Hood standard than Michael Martin. He was no drinker or gambler; indeed, he seems to have been a deeply religious man who had a family in Philadelphia. Also, oral tradition attributed acts of generosity to him. The familiar "Poor Widow" episode is said to have occurred in Mifflin County, where Lewis lent twenty dollars to the unfortunate female and then robbed the bill collector. "Lewis got his twenty dollars back, and forty dollars in addition. He often boasted that the loan of the twenty dollars was one of the best investments he had ever made."

Like Robin Hood, Lewis also shared the qualities of that figure from primitive folklore, the Trickster. Specifically, "in Adams County" he joined a posse searching for himself. While riding over hill and dale with them, he inquired as to each man's name and address. Subsequently he sent word to each posseman, asking him if he had enjoyed the company of "Lewis the Robber." Jesse James pulled the same stunt, so folklore maintains, with a posse in Arkansas.

The requisite social conditions for a Robin Hood legend seem to have existed in Pennsylvania. At least Lewis justified his crimes by referring to such a situation: "If there was any class or description of people in society whom I would sooner have robbed than any other, it was those who held public offices, and under color of law had been guilty of extortion; who had plundered the poor, and cheated the widow and orphan. . . . I conceived that I would be rendering society a service by punishing these official marauders." Like Robin Hood before him, Lewis thus became the interpreter of justice, and claimed to be upholding the true moral law. Some support for his claim is found in the popularity of the "Benefactor" folktales among rural residents of central Pennsylvania. Such tales continued to flourish until the 1920s.

Yet Lewis never achieved national ranking. Perhaps his story did not have enough of the bold and epic quality that distinguishes those of a Robin Hood or a Billy the Kid. He was after all a counterfeiter for a while, and though people can admire the courage and audacity of the bank robber, they have scant regard for a funny-money man. Then, too, some features of the Robin Hood pattern, a betrayal for example, are missing. So Lewis remains a transitional figure lost in a valley between the peaks of outlaw hero-worship in England and America.

Robin Hood's real descendants are the outlaws of the trans-Mississippi West in the period from 1850 to 1900. Here the social conditions were favorable, and there were plenty of candidates. Lawlessness was common during the frontier period because of the great rapidity of settlement, the sparse and scattered population, the universal custom of carrying arms, and the long delay in establishing courts and jails. Social fluidity caused uncertainty as to what was "right" and "wrong," "lawful" or "unlawful." Many Americans had only a dim concept of what was legal, while others thought the law was just hocus-pocus designed to make lawyers rich. The outlaws themselves exploited this confusion to justify their actions. Yet all too often the law was administered on the principle that "might makes right."

In addition, the settlement of the frontier involved a shift from an agricultural toward an industrial economy. Such transitions involve painful adjustments, and those caught up in these changes tend to sympathize with rebels and resisters. The fame of several outlaws seems to be based on the "man versus machine" theme. People identified them with a fast-fading frontier individualism. In the popular view the outlaw had maximal freedom, a freedom increasingly denied to those subject to corporations, banks, and railroads. Symbolic of the outlaw's independence was his horse (albeit a stolen one). Robin Hood had become a folk hero even though he did not use horses, which were impractical in the forests. But the other bandits added to their appeal by being mounted. So in a sense the horse-riding outlaws of this era were the last fit subjects for romantic and legendary literature.

JOAQUIN MURRIETA:
A CALIFORNIA ROBIN HOOD?

Joaquin Murrieta* was the first American outlaw to be consciously molded into the Robin Hood pattern. The result is that the legend, like that of the prototype, strays far from history. Indeed, the actual Murrieta is almost as shadowy a figure as Robin Hood himself. But this has not daunted writers, who have built mountainous biographies from the molehill of facts.

In the Murrieta saga, the setting is Gold Rush California, the heroes are Spanish-speaking "Californios," and the villains are Anglo-American miners. After the discovery of gold at Sutter's Mill in January of 1848, several hundred thousand Yankees spilled into the state, seeking to get rich quick. The unsettled conditions resulting from this influx were conducive to outlawry. Gold dust was a tempting prize, since it could not be traced once stolen. The roads were lonely, the law was far away, and there were many fine horses within easy reach. So American outlaws held up gold shipments, stole horses, and murdered innocent victims during the early 50s. Jack Powers, for example, operated out of Los Angeles during this period, and Tom Bell was a much-feared desperado in the mining country. Yet they never became legendary figures, a status reserved for the native California bandits.

There were over one hundred notorious *bandidos* in the years from 1850 to 1865. The reason for their appearance was related to the economic dislocations accompanying the Gold Rush. The pastoral economy of Spanish and Mexican days, based principally on ranching, came to a rather abrupt end. The ranchers were dispossessed by Yankees, who often made use of the law courts for this purpose. The Spanish Californian found himself unemployed, pushed off the land, and relegated to second-class citizenship under the new order. This bewildering change underlay most of the cultural conflict between *gringo* and "greaser."

When the Yankee miners came to California they found themselves competing with other racial groups, such as the Chinese, the Chileans, and the Mexicans. The result, sad to say,

---

*The name has been spelled in various ways, though the presumed descendants of the family in Sonora use Murrieta, which is the common Spanish spelling.

was discrimination, persecution, and violence directed against these "foreigners." California newspapers between 1849-1852 have numerous reports of American mobs driving Mexicans and others from their claims. There were even attempts to legalize this discrimination. The Foreign Miners' Law of April 13, 1851, levied a tax of $20 per month on aliens and tried to impose a licensing system. The law was repealed within a year, but it symbolized the racial attitudes of the period.

The answer of some Mexicans to this legal and illegal persecution was robbery and murder. The psychology was parallel to that of the Robin Hood legend: crime is justifiable when the law is in the hands of oppressors. The existence of various Californian outlaw bands was commonly attributed to the foreign miners' tax and racial prejudice. Theodore Hittell wrote that "as a natural consequence, being thus rendered destitute of the means of purchasing food and clothing, they became desperate and were driven to theft, robbery and sometimes murder. For several years after persecutions of this kind began, the otherwise waste regions of the upper San Joaquin valley, and particularly that portion of it west of Tulare Lake, were ranged over by gangs amounting in the aggregate to several hundred of Spanish-speaking vagabonds, whose ostensible occupation was running mustangs but whose real business was believed to be robbery and the protection of robbers."

Several of the outlaw leaders seem to have been regarded as Robin Hoods by the Californios. Such was the case with Salomon Pico, a highwayman who operated between Monterey and Los Angeles during 1848-1857. He came from a good family, but resented the injustices committed by the *gringos,* more specifically having been cheated out of his property by them. He vowed revenge and commenced to rob and murder Americans, being protected and perhaps admired by a large part of the Spanish-speaking population. Pico was finally captured by a posse in 1857 and run out of the country. Three years later he was assassinated in Baja California, during a political quarrel.

"Joaquin" himself does not appear on the scene until December of 1852. Even at that he is an extremely elusive character, as befits an outlaw! There are unsolved mysteries concerning his ancestry, appearance, and actions. It is commonly maintained that he was from Sonora, Mexico, but the genealogical connections are impossible to trace. Was he handsome or ugly, squat or cadaverous? No one knew.

The scepticism concerning his identity was expressed by a committee of the state assembly in 1853. It criticized a reward-offer for Joaquin's head on the grounds that "unless the said Joaquin be endowed with supernatural qualities, he could not have been seen at the same time in several places, widely separated from each other. The offer of such reward would be likely to stimulate cupidity, to magnify fancied resemblance, and dozens of heads similar in some respects to that of Joaquin, might be presented for identification." When Governor John Bigler offered a reward of $1,000 for Murrieta, the poster read: "Said Joaquin Carillo is a Mexican by birth, five feet ten inches in height, black hair, black eyes, and of good address." While this description was better than none at all, it was hardly useful in distinguishing Murrieta from several thousand other Californios. All portraits of him are based on conjectures about what he *should* have looked like.

Yet some information has come to light which indicates that there was an actual man behind the legend. Contemporary newspapers record a series of crimes apparently committed by a bold, brutal, but very much alive outlaw. The papers usually referred to this desperado simply as "Joaquin," which seems to have been a generic name for all Californio bandits. Various last names were assigned to him, including Valenzuela, Carillo, and Botellier, but Murrieta seems to be the best bet.

The first newspaper reference appeared on December 15, 1852. The San Francisco *Alta California* mentioned "Joaquin Murieta" as one of the suspects in the theft of over a hundred horses from the White & Courtney corral in San Gabriel on November 25th. Murrieta evidently needed the animals to make a get-away from what was for him a dangerous situation. On the night of November 7th, General Joshua Bean was murdered near the San Gabriel Mission. Bean had been the leader of the local Vigilance Committee, which was trying to apprehend Mexican rustlers as well as stop Indian raids. Murrieta was one of those accused of the murder.

A trial was held, at which a woman named Ana Benites swore on the Bible that Joaquin had been in her arms the night of the killing. Although she thus alibied Joaquin, naming one Cipriano Sandoval as the murderer, Ana revealed also that he was anything but the tender lover that biographers later represented him to be. She testified that he had threatened to rip her guts if she said anything to the Yankees. Despite the alibi, Joaquin decided to make tracks from Los Angeles, since the Vigilantes were taking out other of the accused Mexicans and hanging them from trees.

The outlaw presumably went north and established himself at Yaqui Camp, a small settlement near San Andreas in Calaveras County. A sudden outburst of murder and horse stealing in the area was attributed to a gang of which he was believed to be the leader. Just who the other gang members were is not known. The names of Manuel "Three-Fingered Jack" Garcia, "Claudio," Reyes Feliz, and Jose Ochova have often been cited, but without verification. At any rate, in late January of 1853 the Calaveras newspapers were reporting numerous depredations by "Joaquin's" band. Local law enforcement, such as it was, could not cope with the outbreak. On the 22nd a five-man posse from San Andreas did run into twelve Mexican outlaws, but had to retreat after a short gun battle. The gang rode on to the Phoenix Quartz Mill, where they shot down two hapless Americans. One wounded *bandido* was finally captured, and admitted (said the *Calaveras Chronicle*) "that he was of Joaquin's party, but not a conspicuous or leading member." Despite this disclaimer, he was hanged.

In response to the murder of the two Americans, hundreds of miner-possemen began scouring Calaveras County. All Mexicans were driven from San Andreas itself, and others coming into the county were turned back at the river crossings. By the first week of February, the gang – apparently feeling that the neighborhood was getting too warm – had moved north to the Jackson area of what is now Amador County. On February 8th they slaughtered six Chinese at Big Bar on the Cosumnes River, taking $6,000 in gold dust. Between the 13th and the 20th, nine more "celestials" were robbed and killed in several raids near the Calaveras River. An American, Joseph Lake, was also found dying from knife and bullet wounds on the 13th. A posse from Jackson followed the outlaws by the trail of corpses they left behind.

In these reports of insane butchery the chasm begins to open between history and legend. The fact that Murrieta killed principally Chinese, contradicts the legend, which tells us that his outlawry was essentially a vendetta against the Anglo-Americans. The outlaw who appears in the records is a vicious killer who attacks the easiest victims. Of the twenty or more people who fell before his guns and knives, only three or four were Americans.

On February 21st, Governor Bigler offered a reward of $1,000 for

Joaquin's head, but still the depredations continued. Posses caught sight of the outlaw band on several occasions, but were unable to catch up with the well-mounted raiders. Joaquin seemed to be everywhere at once, and his reputation for invincibility grew with each atrocity. One newspaper reported that he wore a coat of chain mail which made him immune to bullets. Certainly it became apparent that the bandit had a fairly well-organized operation in the Mother Lode, with a system of lookouts and a remuda of good horses that could be used in escapes. The *bandidos* had the advantage of knowing the land, particularly the hundreds of hidden trails that ran from the San Joaquin valley eastward into the Sierra Nevada and westward to the Coast Range. They must also have had the sympathy of some Spanish-speaking people, who perhaps had no admiration for Joaquin, but who resented the *gringo*.

Inevitably, there was speculation about why Joaquin had become an outlaw. The San Francisco *Herald* of April 16th printed an interview with a *ranchero* near Salinas who said that Murrieta had visited him and during dinner had explained the story of his life. He had come to California from Sonora, Mexico, where he had been raised by a good family and given a decent education. He had been a prospector in the Stanislaus region, until being flogged and driven from his claim by the Americans. He had then become a gambler, but further troubles with Americans had forced him into outlawry. This single-column article became the source of much Murrieta lore. Biographers "improved" the story by adding the rape of his sweetheart (or wife) and the hanging of his half-brother to the list of provocations. Floggings and rapes did occur, and could conceivably turn a man into an outlaw. But only a few sources at the time suggested the alternative explanation: that Joaquin was just an *hombre de vicio* who wanted easy money.

By early March, the gang had moved south once again to Hornitos in Mariposa County. On March 4th, they stole horses from Prescott's ranch. A posse trailed them to a tent near Hornitos, but the outlaws escaped after a nighttime gun battle in which two Americans were wounded. A week later, five Frenchmen were robbed and killed at their camp on Bear Creek near Mariposa. "It is supposed that the assassins belonged to Joaquin's band," said the *Sacramento Union*, "and were, perhaps, headed by the rascal himself."

The Frenchmen episode was the last of Joaquin's depredations in the Southern Mines. He had terrorized the area for about two months, January to March of 1853, compiling a short but bloody record. The Mariposans, of course, did not know the terror had ended. They asked the state legislature to offer a reward of $10,000 for Joaquin, dead or alive. The committee on Military Affairs eventually rejected the proposal on the grounds that bounty hunters might bring in "dozens of heads."

The petitions from Mariposa did result in some state action, however. On May 17th, Governor Bigler signed a bill authorizing a twenty-man company of "California Rangers." They were to be on the state payroll for three months, unless Joaquin was caught before that time. The men would get $150 per month, but the Governor's still-pending reward of $1,000 for Joaquin was to be the principal incentive. The captain of the company was a tough Texan with the incongruous name of Harry Love. The Rangers were not the finest representatives of law and order. They included "Bloodthirsty Charlie" Bloodworth; George Evans, "a noted bad man"; and Jim Norton, "the terrible sailor." Many of them came to violent ends, and Love himself was later killed while mistreating his wife.

For two months the Rangers combed the foothills of the San Joaquin Valley. They recovered a number of stolen animals and caught several suspected Mexican rustlers – but not the one and only Joaquin. Then on the morning of July 25th they found their quarry camped at Arroyo Cantua, just north of modern Coalinga. William Byrnes, the only Ranger who claimed to know what Joaquin looked like, identified him as one of the men in the camp. Immediately firing commenced, and in the running gun battle that followed, the outlaw chief was slain. Three other Mexicans were also killed, one of them being the notorious cutthroat "Three-Fingered Jack." As proof of their exploit, the Rangers cut off Joaquin's head and Jack's mutilated hand, and brought the trophies back to the state capital, preserved in alcohol.*

Captain Love evidently expected to meet with some suspicion, for he took the trouble to collect eighteen affidavits from citizens in various parts of the state, affirming that the head was that of *the* Joaquin Murrieta. (One of the witnesses was a prostitute from San Andreas, which tells us how Joaquin had spent his free time.) The newspapers did indeed start expressing doubts, reporting that the real Joaquin had been seen in San Luis Obispo, in the San Fernando

---

*The head was exhibited around the state in subsequent years and was destroyed in the San Francisco Earthquake of 1906.

Valley, in Sonora, Mexico, and in other locations. The San Francisco *Alto* of August 23rd said, "It affords amusement to our citizens to read the various accounts of the capture and decapitation of the notorious Joaquin Murieta.' The humbug is so transparent that it is surprising any sensible person can be imposed upon by the statements of the affair which have appeared in the prints." One jokester who signed himself "Joaquin Carillo" wrote a letter published in the San Francisco *Herald* of August 19th: "Senor Editors Herald: As my capture or supposed capture seems to be the topic of the day, I will, through your kindness, inform your readers of your valuable paper, that I still retain my head, although it is proclaimed through the presses of your city that I was recently captured."

Nevertheless, Governor Bigler and the legislature were evidently convinced. On August 30th, Love was presented with the $1,000 reward check. The Captain must also have had considerable clout with the legislature, for on May 15, 1854, they passed a special act giving him (and his men) an additional $5,000 for "expenses incurred." Still, the debate about the man killed at Arroyo Cantua continued, and it became incorporated into the legend as an escape-to-Mexico theme. There is no way of proving or disproving the Rangers' claim, since there was never any coroner's examination of the case. The character of Love and his bounty hunters was such that they were accused of having gunned down innocent herders in order to claim the reward. It might also be noted that Joaquin's activities in the Mother Lode had ceased months before the Rangers even got their commissions.

The outlaw who appears in these fragmentary historical records was in no way a Robin Hood. In the first place, he did not last long enough. His California career covered only two months, but the real Robin Hood outlaw proves his skill by remaining at large over a period of years. Second, the true Robin Hood type is supposed to shoot only in "self-defence," and his antagonists are well-armed law officers or other professional warriors. But Murrieta was a tiger-like killer whose principal victims were unarmed Chinese.

Most damaging of all, this outlaw did not really champion the cause of his poor countrymen. In fact, he brought them nothing but grief, for the Americans persecuted all Mexicans in the hysteria following Joaquin's crimes. He may even have robbed his compatriots. The *Tuolumne County Miners' and Business Men's Directory*, published in 1856, said of Joaquin that "at this time [1852] he had not commenced his career of wholesale murder and robbery, but was a 'monte dealer' and had a number of villainous scamps connected with him in fleecing his less informed countrymen and others out of their daily earnings." The bandit did not "take from the [American] rich to give to the [Mexican] poor," as does the classic outlaw. He plundered money from the weak and squandered it on gambling, alcohol, and prostitutes.

In short, the actual Joaquin does not match the portrait that legend was to paint of him. How then did he become another "Robin Hood"? It was done through literary manipulation, by wishful biographers who transformed ugliness into Beauty if not Truth.

ROMANTICIZATION OF JOAQUIN

John Rollin Ridge was the man who put a halo on Joaquin's brow. In 1854, his *Life and Adventures of Joaquin Murieta, the Celebrated California Bandit* was published in San Francisco. It was a paperback potboiler, featuring hairbreadth escapes, swooning maidens, and villainous Americans. There were romantic camp scenes, long-winded declamations by the hero, and improbable feats of derring-do. The effect of the book, done deliberately, was to fit Joaquin into the Robin Hood framework.

Revenge and racial antagonism, the two major themes of the biography, were both part of Ridge's own experience. He had been born in Georgia to a white mother and a Cherokee father. During the 1830s his grandfather and father had supported the removal of the Cherokees to Indian Territory as inevitable. But the "anti-removal" faction never forgave them, and they were both murdered when John Rollin Ridge was twelve years old. So he became embroiled in Cherokee politics, always conscious, as he wrote his cousin Stand Watie, that "there is a deep-seated principle of revenge in me that will never be satisfied until it reaches its object." Unfortunately for Ridge, the Treaty faction was greatly outnumbered, so his dreams went unfulfilled.

Ridge joined the Gold Rush in 1850 and bought a weekly newspaper at Nevada City in the Northern Mines. (It is worth noting that the seller was "Lying Jim" Townsend, one of the West's most famous tall-tale raconteurs.) He drifted into other jobs over the next few years and began writing poetry and essays for various periodicals, sometimes using his Indian name of "Yellow Bird." These efforts are virtually forgotten, however, and only *The Life of Murieta* remains as his literary monument.

The early part of the book is based on the thumbnail sketch of Murrieta printed in the San Francisco *Herald* of April 16, 1853. Ridge adopts the story that Murrieta has been a peaceful miner on the Stanislaus until being flogged by Americans. But Ridge is not satisfied with the flogging alone. He triples the provocation by bringing Joaquin's half-brother and sweetheart into the picture.

Biographers of outlaws always *cherchez la femme,* and when they can't find a Maid Marian in the records, they invent one. The only woman mentioned in the contemporary chronicles was Ana Benites, but her unflattering testimony about Joaquin made her a poor heroine for a romantic biography. So Ridge gives Joaquin a beautiful mistress, Rosita Feliz. The two are living happily together on the Stanislaus, in what is depicted as a California Garden of Eden. But then the American hooligans attack Joaquin, beating him unconscious when he tries to resist, and they rape Rosita. Even this episode is not enough to turn him into an outlaw, near-saint that he is. But a short time afterward another mob near Murphy's Diggings publicly whips Joaquin within an inch of his life and hangs the brother as an alleged horse thief. That does it! As Joaquin explains in a bit of reconstructed conversation: "I am a deep-dyed scoundrel, but so help me God! I was driven to it by oppression and wrong."

From this point on, the revenge theme is carefully developed. One by one, the members of the Murphy's Diggings mob are found with their throats cut. This has been a favorite plot-feature for novelists and scenarists, tapping as it does one of the most primitive of human motives. But the episodes are not authenticated by contemporary sources. They really tell us more about Ridge and his revenge fixation than they do about Joaquin.

The significance of the flogging-rape-hanging story is that if one accepts it, as a sort of major premise, one can also accept Ridge's romantic interpretation of the outlaw. Skeptics say that the flogging explanation is irrelevant, that Murrieta would have become an outlaw anyway just because he was a hard case who could not have lived within the rules of any society, Mexican or Anglo. Furthermore, there is the problem of the other supposed members of the gang: "Three-Fingered Jack," "Claudio," and the rest. *They* were not flogged, and *they* did not see their girlfriend ravished. They are represented as common cutthroats who wanted easy pickings of horses or gold. Only Joaquin, it seems, was "forced" into crime by the Americans. The rather contrived nature of this explanation makes it difficult to swallow – unless one is a born romantic.

The basic trouble is that Ridge's Joaquin is just too good to be true. He is so much nobler than the ferocious killers who make up his band that he ceases to resemble a flesh-and-blood outlaw. He had a "generous and noble nature," and a "frank and cordial bearing which distinguished him and made him beloved by all with whom he came in contact." He is particularly considerate of the innocent maidens whom his band captures from time-to-time. In one episode he returns a young woman named Rosalie to her aged mother, after dressing down a wolfish gang-member whose intentions are far from decent. On another occasion he spares a party of American hunters who stumble across his camp. In short, he is depicted as a combination of Jesus Christ and Sir Lancelot.

Evaluation of Ridge's sketch involves an interpretation of the Mexican character. On the one hand, the people are instinctively polite. Many of them remained so even under extreme provocation from aggressive Americans. On the other hand, there was another type of Mexican, exemplified by Pancho Villa or the later California bandit Tiburcio Vasquez, who would shed blood at a moment's notice. Ridge attempts to have it both ways; his Murrieta is gracious but also blood-thirsty. To modern eyes the job is done so clumsily that it lacks credibility, and even some nineteenth century readers saw blemishes in it.

A reviewer in the San Francisco *Chronicle* (August 7, 1854) believed that the *Life* was largely fanciful, but that Murrieta would enjoy reading it, since the reports of his death were probably untrue. Indeed, about the first two-thirds of the book is fiction. Ridge's chronology of Murrieta's early life is a masterpiece of improvisation. He does not cite newspaper reports, but his account fails to match the newspaper record anyway. Rather, there are imaginative versions of authenticated episodes (such as the Bean assassination), invented stories, and borrowed material. In one of Ridge's own stories, Murrieta rescues a comrade at a court trial by masquerading as a prosperous merchant. (Shades of Robin Hood at Nottingham!) In another, Joaquin is in a saloon at Mokelumne Hill when he hears a braggart denouncing the outlaw. Whereupon he jumps up on a table and shouts, "I am Joaquin! If there is any shooting to do, I am in." The crowd stands paralyzed as he then walks calmly out the door.

Much of the borrowed material is from the San Francisco *Herald* article, such as a story that at Stockton Joaquin had seen a reward poster offering five thousand dollars for him dead or alive. Amidst a crowd of onlookers, he nonchalantly writes across it, "I will give $10,000 – Joaquin." (The historian asks: when was $5,000 ever offered for Joaquin?) Ridge fills in the gaps between these exploits with lavishly detailed camp scenes, where Joaquin "lounges on the luxurious lap of his mistress."

Only about the last third of the book, including the account of Murrieta's death and decapitation, is solidly factual. Here, Ridge, like a psychotic with moments of clarity, finally bases his narrative upon actual occurrences. At least his text matches the contemporary newspaper reports with reasonable accuracy. Thus the *Life and Adventures* is a strange hybrid, like most of the other Murrieta literature that was to follow. Not quite a historical novel, it should perhaps be called a "fictionalized biography."

The book was not an immediate success. Ridge wrote to Stand Watie that "I expected to have made a great deal of money off my book, my life of Joaquin Murieta (a copy of which I have sent you), but my publishers, after selling 7,000 copies and putting the money in their pockets, fled, bursted up, tee totally smashed, and left me, with a hundred others, to whistle for our money." There is reason to believe that Ridge was exaggerating his financial difficulties, perhaps to wangle a loan from Cousin Stand. Yet in the long run the little volume was more influential than Ridge could ever have expected. It became the master blueprint for the Murrieta legend.

The biography, by making the outlaw's name better known, contributed to folklore about him among the Anglo-Americans. In 1855, a topical song entitled "Joaquin the Horse Thief" was printed by John A. Stone in his *Put's Original California Songster.* Sung to the tune of "Now I Warn All You Darkies Not to Love Her," the text presents a disjointed and moralizing account of the bandit's career:

> I suppose you have heard all the talkin'
> Of the very noted horse-thief, Joaquin;
> He was caught in Calaveras, but he couldn't stand the joke,
> So the Rangers cut his head off and have got it now in soak.
>
> Now I warn everybody not to ramble,
> Never drink, never fight, never gamble,
> For you'll never have a cent, all your money will be spent,
> And you to Sacramento to the prison brig be sent.
>
> They took Three-Fingered Jack and cut his hand off,
> Then the Rangers drove the rest of his band off.
> They took the head and hand and had it well preserved,
> And the Rangers got the credit, which they much deserved.
>
> Joaquin to the mountains was advancing.
> When he saw Lola Montez a-dancing;
> When she danced the spider dance, he was bound to run her off,
> And he'd feed her eggs and chickens, make her cackle, crow and cough.

Joaquin, just before he was taken,
Killed a Chinaman and then stole his bacon;
Then he went to Sonora, where he killed eleven more,
And the big Digger Indian, which made him twenty-four.

You have heard of the steel he wore around him,
I will tell you what it was when they found him,
'Twas a long-tom iron to protect him in his crimes,
And they swore by the holes he'd been shot a thousand
times.

Now the head, it can be seen at Sacramento,
But to have it there they never did intend to;
For he fought like the de--l, while they had half a show,
But the Rangers put an end to the terror of Mexico.

It is interesting that this song was carried back to Michigan by
some returning miners, who called the character "Wakken." This is
clearly a phonetic rendering by Americans who were unfamiliar
with Spanish spelling and who probably heard the song around a
campfire rather than reading Stone's text.

The biography also inspired the first purely literary portrayal of
the outlaw. This was Charles E.B. Howe's *A Dramatic Play Entitled
Joaquin Murieta De Castillo, the Celebrated Bandit,* published at San
Francisco in 1858. The five-act play was clearly based on Ridge's
Life, although the sweetheart Rosita is renamed Belloro and there
are other minor alterations. The play was aimed at Anglo audiences, and was evidence of Murrieta's rather rapid elevation to
legendary status among that audience.

Ridge's book continued to attract more readers over the next few
years. Proof of its popularity lies in the fact that a "Third Edition"
was brought out in 1871, four years after the author's death. The
few changes that Ridge made in this edition, such as sharpening the
persecution theme, indicate a deliberate intention to create a Robin
Hood figure. It seems unlikely that there was ever a "Second Edition." Ridge and his publisher seem to have regarded a competitive
biography issued in 1859 as such a close copy of Ridge's work that it
was virtually a second edition. Another possibility is that Ridge was
actually the ghost writer of this anonymously authored plagiarism.
Entitled "Joaquin Murieta, the Brigand Chief of California," it was
run in ten consecutive issues of a San Francisco newspaper called
The California Police Gazette. It was then published as a pamphlet,
which was illustrated (as was the newspaper series) with woodcuts
by the noted artist Charles Christian Nahl.

Portrait of John Rollin Ridge. He portrayed Joaquin Murrieta as a California Robin Hood. Courtesy Society of California Pioneers.

The *Gazette* writer alters the sequence of events somewhat, but he does follow the Ridge text pretty closely. Joaquin is again born in Sonora, is "well-educated," and is initially of a peaceable disposition. At Mokelumne Hill he jumps up on that same monte table, this time shouting, "I am Joaquin, I dare you to shoot." At Stockton, on the reward poster offering $5,000 for his head, he again writes,

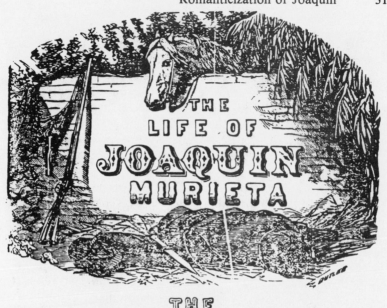

Joaquin Murrieta as depicted by Charles C. Nahl, on the cover of the *California Police Gazette* biography, published in 1859. Courtesy University of California at Los Angeles.

"I will give $10,000 — Joaquin." But for all this copying, there are some imaginative variations. The author tampers with the girlfriend, Rosita Feliz. Her name is changed to Carmela, her status altered from sweetheart to wife, and her rape is immediately followed by her death. But within a few pages Joaquin is given a girlfriend to replace the wife; she is called Clarina. The substitution of Carmela and Clarina for Rosita caused a lot of migraine hadaches for later writers, who weren't sure just what name to give to Joaquin's women.

Some of the new episodes in the *Gazette* version became part of the pseudo-folklore attached to the outlaw's name. Murrieta's generosity seems to have increased each year since 1853, a familiar feature in Robin Hood traditions. For example, Joaquin holds up the Hangtown (Placerville) stage, but he returns a golden cross to a Mexican woman passenger. There is also a reference to his having buried a treasure near Hangtown; later literary sources were to attribute several legends to him. These touches indicate that if Ridge was, in fact, the *Gazette* ghost writer, he did a somewhat more professional job with this version.

By 1859, the pattern of the Murrieta legend had been pretty well established. Later novels and histories were essentially variations on the "classic" sources, Ridge's *Life and Adventures* or the *Gazette* story, sometimes on a gratuitous splicing of the two. Novelists seem to have preferred the *Gazette* version. Henry Llewellyn Williams in *Joaquin, (the Claude Duval of California)*, an 1865 dime novel, followed the Carmela-Clarina story line. So did Joseph E. Badger in his 1881 dime novel, *Joaquin the Terrible; The True History of Three Bitter Blows That Changed an Honest Man to a Bitter Demon.* The three blows are the rape of his wife Carmela, the hanging of his half-brother, and the whipping that he got at Murphy's Diggings.

Historians relied upon Ridge's interpretation. In their massive histories of California published in the 1880s, both Hubert Howe Bancroft and Theodore Hittell gambled that Ridge was reliable. Their sections on Murrieta are basically abstracts from the "Third Edition," with some polishing of the narrative. Bancroft, for example, has Murrieta die at twenty-one, while Ridge says he was twenty-two. (All writers from Ridge on assume that Murrieta was a young man in 1853, but there is no proof of this and he may have been in his forties.) Bancroft states that "many a Pastoral Californian" believed Murrieta had been a Robin Hood, but unfortunately he did not support his conclusions with proof. Through these reputable works, which are still standard sources for state history, Ridge's pipe dreams were made known to following generations.

The decades from 1870 to 1930 saw occasional items on Murrieta. Most of these were articles in California newspapers or reminiscences in the county histories. Much of the material consisted of "wild stories and improbable narrations." In their reminiscences, the "old timers," writing twenty-five years or so after Murrieta's death, recalled that they had known him before he became a notorious outlaw. One rancher said that he had saved the life of Joaquin, and that subsequently the bandit had called off a robbery after recognizing his savior. Another settler said that he had once given Joaquin eight thousand dollars to deliver to a friend. In a story printed in 1876, a doctor remembered that he had paid several visits to Joaquin's mountain hideout, and had seen the desperado put on disguises as an old man and as a young girl.

There were also a few more ambitious attempts to retell the Murrieta saga. These were produced by intellectuals, such as Charles Park and Joseph Gollomb, who seemed intent on remaking the outlaw into their own image but who would have been horrified had they met a real bandit. In 1912, Park (under the name of "Carl Gray") published a novel entitled *Plaything of the Gods.* A sentimental story, it had the teen-aged Joaquinm studying to be a priest: "he's taking Philosophia Scholastical, Dogmatic Theology and Ballerini's Moral Theology and Fouard's Life of Christ." The student is unjustly accused of being a horse thief, but he escapes from jail and moves up to the mining country. There, after his wife Carmela is dishonored, he turns into the vengeful-yet-still-chivalrous outlaw of the Ridge tradition. Park was so taken by his hero that he does not permit him to die by gunfire at Arroyo Cantua. Instead, he drowns while boating on a pleasant lake!

Gollomb relied on the Police Gazette's "Carmela-Clarina" plot in his book *Master Highwayman* (1927). After "much hunting in dust-covered records," Gollomb found that Murrieta had been born in Sonora to parents who had given him a decent education. In fact, he retained his love of books as long as he lived, and in camp he read Cervantes and Racine! Gollomb seemed to realize that he had an uphill fight in trying to make his bookish outlaw a believable figure. As he says, "I was astonished to find that he is today so little known." Preposterous as Gollomb's essay was, it was cited as a historical source in the *Dictionary of American Biography* sketch of

Murrieta.

If Murrieta was not familiar to most Americans outside California during this period, he did have an audience in the Spanish-speaking world. Spain, Chile, and Mexico all had published pirated translations of either Ridge or the *Gazette* story — eleven separate editions all together. A popular version was Ireneo Paz, *Vida Y Aventuras del Mas Celebre Bandido Sonorense Joaquin Murrieta.* Published at Mexico City in 1908, this biography was a virtual copy of the 1859 *Gazette* story. Several editions of this book were also issued in Los Angeles for the large Spanish-speaking population there. And, incredible as it may seem, the Los Angeles edition was retranslated into English by Francis P. Belle, and published at Chicago in 1925 for the Anglo market!

Despite his shortcomings as a Robin Hood, Murrieta seems to have been regarded as a hero in Mexico. As early as 1853, G.F. von Tempsky, a professional traveler who spoke Spanish, was told by Mexicans that Joaquin was still alive in Sonora and that "his countrymen adored him." In 1872, an American engineer Albert K. Owen, wrote (in his diary) of having seen a play in Sonora which was based on Joaquin's exploits. "It meets the applause of the Mexicans," Owen reported. The play, by an actor-author named Don Gabutti, was probably a reworked version of Charles E.B. Howe's *A Dramatic Play Entitled Joaquin Murieta de Castillo.* It appears that most of the Murrieta "folklore" in the Spanish-speaking community ultimately derives from some printed source — and an Anglo author.

Chile has also claimed Joaquin as a native son. The Chilean case is based on the *Police Gazette* biography. This had been translated into French by Robert Heyenne in 1862, and the French version was in turn the basis of a Spanish edition issued in Santiago de Chile about 1870. Fourteen editions of *El Bandido Chileno, Joaquin Murieta en California* were published over the next twenty years. In 1926, Ignacio Herrera attempted to legitimize Joaquin's Chilean ancestry in a pamphlet, *Joaquin Murrietta, El Bandido Chileno en California,* which maintained that the outlaw had been born in Santiago in 1830. Then, in 1960, the Chilean poet Pablo Neruda wrote a play based on the same supposition: *Splendor and Death of Joaquin Murieta, Chilean Bandit Unjustly Killed in California on July 23, 1853.* A fanciful story emphasizing the terrorism and discrimination against Latins in the United States, the drama is essentially a vehicle for Communist propaganda.

MODERN MURRIETA LEGEND

In the 1930s, the Murrieta legend suddenly blossomed like a tropical flower. It was a great decade for outlaws, both living and legendary. Perhaps in times of trouble, like the Great Depression, some people naturally seek escape in the stories of Romantic Bandits.

The key book in this period was a new biography written by Walter Noble Burns. The best thing about the work was its title, *The Robin Hood of El Dorado.* Burns kept drumming upon the Robin Hood-Murrieta parallel; in fact, he almost worked it to death. His third chapter, entitled "Robin Hood and His Merry Men," is close to parody:

> The murderous robber... is a protector of women. He robs the rich and gives freely to the poor. He feasts, he dances, he toasts his merry men in bumpers of wine, he takes his ease under the greenwood tree. He is the Robin Hood of El Dorado. The live oaks, digger pines and manzanita thickets of the Sierra foothills are his Sherwood Forest; and Three-Fingered Jack, Claudio, Gonzalez, Valenzuela — as atrocious knaves as ever cut a throat — lack only jerkins of Lincoln green, long bows and cloth-yard arrows to be the Little John, Allan-a-dale, Will Scarlet and Friar Tuck of his roystering crew.

Burns' book ran to 304 pages, compared with Ridge's 90. The difference is accounted for by what one reviewer called "a lot of ginger-bread work." Among the digressions are material on the social history of the period; the reprinting of some of the old-timers' reminiscenses; and passages recording the "philosophical reflections" of the outlaws as they go about their activities. There were also a number of newly invented episodes, such as Joaquin's rescue of various comrades, that were put in to strengthen the Robin Hood concept.

Burns had to grapple with the inconsistencies between the Ridge and *Gazette* versions, but he came up with some ingenious solutions. Joaquin's Rosita and Carmela are blended into one wife, Rosita Carmel Feliz, and we are given her complete genealogy in Sonora. After she is murdered "at Saw Mill Flat," Joaquin acquires a girlfriend named Clarito Valero, and the by-now dubious reader is also given her life story.

The last chapter, entitled "Strange Tales," does recapitulate some of the traditional escape-to-Mexico folklore. Such stories were an important part of the legend from the beginning, and the San Francisco newspapers had printed several of them in 1853. Literary works also helped popularize the idea that Joaquin had escaped to Sonora. In 1882, for example, one Marcus Stewart had published a poem entitled "Rosita: A California Tale," which described the outlaw as living peacefully "far south of California's strand" after his supposed death. Burns simply rejuvenated some of these well-worn speculations.

Biographers are usually judged by how accurately they record the life of the subject. But such a measurement seems meaningless in the case of Joaquin Murrieta. There are simply not enough facts about him to warrant a full-length biography. So the only question is how good a story the biographer tells. Measured by this standard, Burns ranks high. His book was written with genial good humor, as if the readers were not really expected to believe it. (However, it was convincing enough so that one reference work, the *Columbia Encyclopedia,* cites it as a historical source.) Published at the bottom of the Depression in 1932, it was still popular enough to go through several editions. And, as ultimate proof of story values, it was sold to Metro-Goldwyn-Mayer for filming.

The motion picture used Burns' title and was more or less based on the book. Released in 1936, it starred Warner Baxter as an idealized Murrieta. The scenes at the outlaw camp in "Lost Valley" depicted a California equivalent of Sherwood Forest, with Joaquin passing the time by strumming a Spanish guitar. The script has him absolved of all fault for his outlawry. The Yankee villains, played by the most evil-faced actors in Hollywood, murder Joaquin's wife. He then hunts down and slays them one by one. This was an early "message" film, and European and Latin American film critics have always been interested in its racial-discrimination theme. For example, Jean-Louis Rieupeyrout in *Le Western* praised the director (William Wellman) for "stigmatizing the errors in a troubled period of the American past."

Other contributions to the legend popped up in the wake of the biography and the motion picture. They also were in a special category between historical fiction and fictionalized biography. Dan Coolidge's *Gringo Gold* (1939) was technically a novel, but the author maintains that "while written in the form of a novel, it probably contains more truth than some of the books published as histories." The story was based on material supplied by Mrs. Nellie J. Abbott, the daughter of Ranger Bill Byrnes. "While fighting with the Texas Rangers in the war with Mexico, Byrnes was taken prisoner and sent to Caborca, Sonora, where he went to school with Joaquin and Rosita, who later became Murrieta's wife." That may be, but the novel does not incorporate any fresh material on Joaquin. It is essentially a blend of the narratives by Ridge, Charles Park, and others. Nor is the chronology synchronous with the contemporary records; for example, the murder of General Bean comes *after* Joaquin's depredations in the Mother Lode.

In 1938, a Los Angeles publisher brought out a volume that contributed to the legend, even though its title was *The Truth About Murrieta*. The text was composed of stories collected across the years from both Californios and Anglos, some of whom claimed to have known Murrieta. This was presumably folk history, passed on from one generation to the next by word of mouth ever since 1853. Actually, most of the accounts derive from Ridge, Burns, or one of the Spanish-language biographies. For example, one woman said that Joaquin had made friends with her, and then in a subsequent stage holdup had returned a gold cross and called off the robbery when he recognized her. This is a somewhat more elaborate version of an anecdote first printed in the 1859 *Police Gazette* biography.

On the other hand, some of the stories may have an independent origin, since they are the kind told about all Robin Hood outlaws. This is particularly the case with Joaquin-is-still-alive tales, which were rooted in the uncertainty about the identity of the outlaw. The Californios might logically be expected to adopt such tales, for over the years his crimes were forgotten and he gradually became a benefactor hero. The belief that he escaped to Mexico is a form of deification, since it implies that he would return some day to champion the rights of the downtrodden.

The real "truth about Murrieta," however, is that printed biographies rather than family traditions, are the ultimate source of most lore among the Spanish-speaking population. For example, the *corrido* is a popular form of topical song, and it features outlaws like Pancho Villa and Gregorio Cortez. But the lone "Corrido de Joaquin Murieta" is of late origin, and reflects the literary evolution of the legend rather than folk composition. Similarly, a sampling of fourth- and fifth-grade children in Los Angeles revealed that what they knew about Joaquin was derived not from family traditions but from a textbook selection they had read.

Buried-treasure stories do not seem to have circulated until the twentieth century, again reflecting literary influences. But such stories inevitably become attached to famous outlaws, and they persist because they are based on the powerful motives of hope and credulity. The favored location for "Joaquin's treasure" is the western foothills of the San Joaquin Valley, but other sites from Placerville to Los Angeles have also been mentioned. A typical story was printed in the *Los Angeles Times* of April 9, 1928. Under the title, "Gold Cave Tales Revived," it is reported that one Manuel Lopez had a map purporting to show the location of Murrieta's treasure: a cave in the Merced River canyon. Another story in the Los Angeles *Daily News* of June 28, 1948, said that Mexican-Americans had for many years been trying to dig up Joaquin's gold in the City Terrace district, but had found only old coke bottles.

Joaquin attacking the Hangtown Stage.

Murrieta holding up a stage. From the 1859 *California Police Gazette* biography. Courtesy University of California at Los Angeles.

Warner Baxter as Joaquin in a scene from *The Robin Hood of El Dorado.*
Courtesy Metro-Goldwyn-Mayer.

At the end of the Thirties' decade, then, the Robin Hood
stereotype had been well established. The murderous character of
the original *bandido* had been diluted in the flood of romantic
literature. As the *Sacramento Union* headlined a Murrieta story
(March 23, 1941): "Time Softens Features of State's Early Day Bandits." Judging from the books and the film, his crimes had been the
most excusable in the history of mankind.

Paradoxically, in the post-World War II period, Joaquin acquired
a swollen reputation for meanness. Like the old debate over
California and Florida oranges, it was asserted that he was a lot
worse than the outlaws of other regions. "As bandits and toughmen
go," wrote Stanford Calderwood in 1947, "Jesse James and John Dillinger look like a couple of overrated amateurs when compared to
Joaquin Murrieta." He had "personally killed dozens of men" during
a three-year reign of terror. These were bold statements indeed
regarding an outlaw about whom so little was really known. Ridge
and Burns, between them, had tailored such a tight straight jacket

that later authors had no chance to wriggle loose.

In 1950, Rockwell D. Hunt included an essay on the bandit along with those of other famous men of the state in a book entitled *California's Stately Hall of Fame.* "Any history of California would be incomplete without the story of Joaquin Murieta," wrote Doctor Hunt. This assessment was confirmed by the frequency with which the outlaw's name appeared in popular historical and literary works over the next two decades. In addition, Murrieta lore became almost a minor industry in California. Many of the old mining towns played up the outlaw legend in their tourist promotion efforts. Hornitos advertises that it was once frequented by "the West's most famous outlaw." Volcano boasts of a large tree called "Murieta's Roost" from which the outlaw watched for posses. At Murphy's, tourists may buy color postcards bearing what is allegedly a photograph of Murrieta. Near Angel's Camp there is a summit called Joaquin's Lookout, and a supposed hideout named Joaquin's Cave. (There is another Joaquin's Lookout in Fresno County, near the Arroyo Cantua). The various "Joaquin" landmarks are almost as numerous, though no more credible, than the "Robin Hood" hideaways in Old England. The bandits who appear in contemporary reports were constantly on the move; to have stayed in a cave for more than a day or so would have been suicidal.

Some kill-joy critics did not think that Murrieta was historically important, and they even denied that he had existed. Joseph Henry Jackson, literary editor of the San Francisco *Chronicle,* wrote in the introduction to a reissue of Ridge's *Life and Adventures* (1955) that "there wasn't a Murieta — at any rate not much of a Murieta." He based his conclusion on a careful study of the legend's evolution. Jackson was not a popular man in the old mining towns, where the Murrieta lore is taken quite seriously. Many people there and in the San Joaquin Valley had no doubts that Joaquin had been an actual person. One Valley historian published an article in 1962 whose title, "Sold on Murrieta," exemplified their belief. Among those the author interviewed was a 107-year-old woman who claimed that she had cooked meals for Joaquin.

Hollywood too helped to keep the legend alive when Warner Brothers brought out *Murieta* in 1965. Jeffrey Hunter portrayed a Joaquin who was a sweet and gentle Mexican peasant — until a vicious gang of Anglos violates and then murders his wife Rosita. He then becomes a professional gambler and a skilled gunman.

This quick transformation is as unconvincing in the film as it is in the legend generally. Joaquin's friend [sic] Captain Harry Love tries to help him get back on the right side of the law, but the inveterate Anglo enemies continue their harassment and make this impossible. Joaquin still promises Love that he will stop the raids, but the gang continues them under the leadership of Three-Fingered Jack. Joaquin is on his way to surrender when Love kills him.

The greater cultural self-awareness of ethnic minorities would seem likely to enhance the popularity of the Murrieta legend. Yet, ironically, the original legend was manufactured by Anglo-Saxon writers, or Anglo-Indian to be perfectly accurate about Ridge's ancestry. It is thus not a grass-roots tradition as far as la raza are concerned. They have made authentic folk heroes of such twentieth century rebels as Pancho Villa and Gregorio Cortez, who defied the Yankees and got away with it. (Cortez outwitted and outfought the Texas Rangers along the Rio Grande in 1901.) Both of them are glorified in folktales and corridos.

Murrieta, on the other hand, was more or less preempted by Anglo-American writers and movie-makers. On the screen he was always played by Anglo actors. In 1971, NBC did offer a television movie, Desperate Mission, that was the pilot of a projected series starring Mexican-born Ricardo Montalban as Joaquin. But the series did not sell, much to Montalban's disappointment.* The film was a pure adventure tale with no pretentions to biographical accuracy. Joaquin is cosmopolitan ("I speak four languages") and compassionate. He is so polite, so sensitive, so idealized that the film lacked any of the earthiness which is the earmark of a convincing outlaw story. The Mexican heroine made a half-hearted reference to the bandit's legendary status when she remarked at the end of the film: "He will come back when we need him."

For the Anglo-American audience, Murrieta never achieved top ranking among the Robin Hoods. His name became better known after Burns's book appeared in 1932. But he has always been well behind Jesse James and Billy the Kid, who are nationally recognized. Perhaps the theme of revenge, important as it is in outlaw narrative, cannot by itself carry a legend. Perhaps a minority-group figure, no matter how sympathetically portrayed, cannot really achieve broad appeal.

---

*Montalban said in the Hollywood Reporter that the series would have given non-Mexicans an unstereotyped view of Murrieta: "To the Mexican he was a hero, a wronged Robin Hood, their avenger."

Then, too, it may be that Murrieta lost credibility through type-association with such fictional characters as the Cisco Kid and Captain Zorro. The Cisco Kid was created by the nineteenth century author, O. Henry. As developed in a 1930s radio serial and in several films starring first Warner Baxter and then Cesar Romero, he remained an outlaw but was essentially a comic figure. His sidekick, Pancho, was the stereotyped Mexican buffoon: "Cisco, the Sheriff, he is getting closer!" Captain Zorro, "the masked avenger of old California," was born in a novel by Johnston McCulley. Two screen versions of *The Mark of Zorro* featured Douglas Fairbanks, Sr. (1920) and Tyrone Power (1939), and in the 1960s Guy Williams played the role in a Walt Disney television series. Zorro was always dashing and romantic; clearly a figure from Fantasyland. So the public perhaps assumed that all Spanish-surname bandits were purely fictional characters.

Still the Murrieta legend has great vitality. The parallels with the Robin Hood prototype virtually guarantee its perpetuation. Joaquin's presumed service to the "cause" of his abused compatriots matches Robin Hood's concern for fellow-yeomen. His robberies of the *gringo* compare with the Hood gang's exactions from churchmen and nobles. The tales of his escape to Mexico, of his various cave-hideouts, and other local legends match similar materials in the English outlaw cycle. And, finally, both came to be representative and generic stories, rather than specific and individual ones. Like Robin Hood, Joaquin became a composite outlaw. He is the avenger of all those Mexicans who were flogged, lynched, or cheated during the Gold Rush era. His "biography" teaches a valuable lesson about racial discrimination, and sheds light on the unsettled conditions of frontier days. It makes a good story which will undoubtedly be retold in additional biographies, novels, and films. Since the historian can do little to recall the legend for factual repairs, he might as well relax and enjoy it along with the rest of the audience.

JESSE JAMES:
GUERRILLA FIGHTER TO OUTLAW

There are two sets of renowned James brothers in American history, but Frank and Jesse seem to be better known than William and Henry. Jesse Woodson James has good claim to being this country's archetypal outlaw. He lasted long enough, seemed to personify the rebel-with-a-cause, and had a catchy name. (What if Jesse had been christened Orville Scruggins?) It is conventional to call him "the American Robin Hood," but his legend has swollen to such dimensions that perhaps it is time to call Robin Hood the "Jesse James of Old England."

The James family seems to have been trouble-prone from the start. Jesse was born in Clay County, Missouri, on September 5, 1847 (Frank being five years older) to Robert and Zarelda James. The father was a Baptist minister, a well-educated man with intellectual interests, and one can only speculate about what "the Boys" might have become had he lived. But for unexplained reasons he went to the California goldfields in 1850 and died there from cholera. So Jesse was brought up by his iron-willed mother and a pleasantly ineffectual stepfather, Dr. Reuben Samuel. Some early writers tried to protray the two brothers in childhood as sadistic little monsters, who "manifested especial delight in punishing dumb animals." But they seem to have been no different from thousands of other youths raised in farming communities during that era.

The Civil War, however, was a catalyst for the James brothers as for many others. Mrs. Samuel was a slaveholder, and there was never any doubt about the family's commitment to the Southern cause. Yet Missouri remained in the Union despite the efforts of secessionists. The regular Confederate forces were driven out of the state in 1862. The pro-Southern effort was henceforth conducted by guerrilla bands, which burned bridges, cut telegraph lines, and attacked both Federal patrols and Unionist irregulars ("Jayhawkers"). Many of these bands seem to have been more interested in plunder than in politics. When Fletcher Taylor, a lieutenant of the notorious William Clarke Quantrill, came recruiting in Clay County, his slogan was "Join Quantrill and rob the banks."

Big brother Frank certainly responded to the opportunity with alacrity. An item in the Liberty (Missouri) *Tribune* of August 7, 1863, shows what he was up to: "Three Southern Gentlemen in Search of Their Rights — On the morning of the 6th of August, Franklin James, with two others of the same stripe stopped David Mitchell, on his road to Leavenworth, about 6 miles west of Liberty, and took from him $125, his pocket knife, and a pass he had from the Provost Marshal to cross the plains. This is one of the 'rights' these men are fighting for." A couple of weeks later, on the 21st, Frank took part in Quantrill's retaliatory raid on Lawrence, Kansas. (Cole Younger, the James Boys' future partner-in-crime, was also on this raid.) The guerrillas killed one hundred fifty men and boys and burned down most of the buildings in the "abolitionist" town. Frank undoubtedly participated in enough other bushwhacking expeditions during the war to harden him forever to the sight of blood.

Jesse James seems to have entered the guerrilla bands in the fall of 1863, when he was sixteen years old. Folk tradition rather than any printed record tells us that it was "persecution" by the Unionist militia that drove him into the bushwhacking business. The militia in Clay County was suspicious of Dr. and Mrs. Samuel because of their outspoken secessionist views and their alleged assistance to various guerrillas. A squad visited the Samuel farm and attempted to make them talk. Dr. Samuel had a rope put around his neck and was dangled from a tree several times. Mrs. Samuel was insulted, shoved around, and reportedly put in jail for two weeks on a charge of aiding the enemy. Jesse was plowing a field when the militiamen appeared and began beating him with rope ends. It seems likely that Jesse would have joined the guerrillas anyway. But this "beating" story became an important part of the James legend, being offered as the justification for his eventual commitment to outlawry.

There is no doubt that Jesse was a valued member of the independent band led by "Bloody Bill" Anderson. Among other engagements, he was present at the Centralia (Missouri) massacre of September 26, 1864. The town was looted, and twenty-five unarmed Union soldiers on furlough were shot down. An army column under Major A.V.E. Johnson pursued the raiders, but was virtually annihilated. Many years later, Frank James admitted to a newspaper reporter that Jesse himself had killed the major.

Jesse not only shot but was shot at, and on three occasions the op-

Guerrillas. Fletcher Taylor, Frank James, and Jesse James (left to right).
Courtesy State Historical Society of Missouri.

position scored. In early August of 1864, he was shot through the chest by a Unionist named Heisinger, but recovered fast enough to take part in the Centralia raid. In another engagement at about the same time, the tip of a finger on his left hand was blown off. Then, in May of 1865, some Union soldiers fired on him as he rode into Lexington, Missouri, under a white flag. He was again hit in the chest, and this time it took him a long time to recover. The scars from all these war wounds were the means by which Jesse James was identified when he was killed by Bob Ford in 1882.

The wounding of Jesse James as he tried to surrender exemplified the murky situation in which the guerrillas found themselves at war's end. While many surrendered to the military authorities and then resumed their civilian lives, others never did so. The bone-deep hatreds engendered by all the bushwhacking were not easily forgotten, and some of the Southern men who surfaced too quickly were shot or hanged by vengeful vigilantes. Jesse James always argued that if he ever turned himself in, he would be shot like a rabid dog.

Even veterans of the regular Confederate Army had a difficult time in Missouri. The state government established after the war was run by Radical Republicans. They passed laws barring former Confederates from voting, holding office, sitting on juries, or practicing most professions. This made adjustment hard for men who wished to resume their old lives. Some of the ex-guerrillas, however, were never willing or able to become storekeepers or farmers. Because of the excitement and easy money in a horse-and-pistol career, they simply became "civilian" guerrillas.

It took almost six months for Jesse's chest wound to heal. Part of this time he was nursed by his cousin, Zerelda Mimms, whom he was eventually to marry in 1874. The two brothers lived for several years on the family farm near Kearney, in Clay County. They had all the outward appearance of respectability. Jesse joined the Mount Olive Baptist church, was a teetotaler, and seemed to be a hard-working farmer. But those two years with the guerrillas had left their indelible imprint on the young man. He simply was unable to face a lifetime of walking behind the plow. As an unsympathetic writer (Emerson Hough) was to say of the James Brothers: "they preferred the ways of robbery and blood in which they had begun."

The brothers' first venture into peacetime banditry was the robbery of a bank at nearby Liberty, Missouri. On February 13, 1866, ten well-armed and well-mounted men rode into town. Two of them entered the Clay County Savings Bank, and cashier Greenup Bird found himself looking down the barrel of a Colt six-shooter. The outlaws stuffed $60,000 in currency and government bonds into burlap sacks which they carried. The leader seemed to have a primordial sense of humor, for as he locked the cashier into the vault he remarked that "all Birds should be caged." The whole gang then galloped out of town, firing pistols and giving rebel yells. A local college student, seventeen-year-old George Wymore, happened to be standing in the street. One of the outlaws fired at him, and he fell dead with four closely spaced bullet holes in the chest.

The local citizens did not think that the outlaws were Robin Hoods. The *Liberty Tribune* editorialized that it was "one of the most cold-blooded murders and heavy robberies on record" and went on to pray that "the villains may be overhauled and brought to the end of a rope." But Mr. Bird was unable to identify the robbers, although none of them had worn masks. A local farmer, Captain Minter, said he had sold grain sacks to Frank and Jesse James the day before the holdup; but he later decided he had been mistaken! Intimidation of witnesses is a familiar aspect of criminal history, but nowhere was it more evident than in post-war Missouri. Talking to the law was like signing one's own death warrant.

Attribution of various robberies to the James gang has been based upon several criteria, including both the techniques used and "guilt by association." Bonds taken from the Liberty bank were sold by former members of "Bloody Bill" Anderson's band. George Shepherd, a well-known confederate of Jesse James, cashed a 1,000-dollar note in Memphis, Tennessee. As for the technique, it was a natural evolution from guerrilla operations. The shooting and yelling to terrorize townspeople was almost a replay of any Quantrill or Anderson raid.

The James brothers were also suspected of the Russellville, Kentucky, bank robbery on March 20, 1868. Five gunmen forced the manager to put $12,000 into the usual grain sacks, and then escaped after a shoot-out. If the brothers were involved, some of the loot may have been used to send Jesse by sea to California, where he stayed with an uncle, Dyson W. James, in Paso Robles, for about a month, lounging in the sulphur baths at that resort. But Missouri was always home, and he was back there by the end of the year.

Jesse James in 1874. Courtesy Division of Manuscripts, University of Oklahoma Library.

Frank and Jesse did not achieve notoriety as bank robbers until 1869. On December 7th, the bank at Gallatin, Missouri, was robbed by two men who killed cashier John Sheets. The horse of one of the bandits bolted, and he had to double up behind his partner to escape. The runaway animal was identified in the Kansas City *Times* as "belonging to a young man named James, whose mother and stepfather live about four miles from Centerville [Kearney], Clay County." The Gallatin *North-Missourian* of December 16th said only that the suspects were "two brothers by the name of James."

These reports indicate that Jesse was not a well-known bandit. But after Gallatin there was little doubt about what his occupation was. Many respectable people in Clay County, including former Confederate soldiers, had nothing to do with the Jameses after this episode. The state government, however, manifested a keen interest in their whereabouts. Governor Joseph McClurg offered $500 for the capture or killing of each man. The murder of an unarmed cashier was a capital offense, punishable by hanging, so the brothers had a compelling reason for keeping their tracks well hidden.

The outlaws remained brazen and audacious despite the pressure from police agencies. The bank at Corydon, Iowa, some one hundred miles northeast of Kearney, was held up on June 3, 1871. Four men believed to have been the James brothers, Cole Younger, and Clell Miller took $12,000 in a few minutes work. It was an easy job, since most of the citizens were attending a speech by the politician, Henry Clay Dean. Indeed, the outlaws stopped at the edge of the crowd and announced that there had been a robbery. Before the startled townsmen could organize pursuit, the bandits were well down the trail to Missouri.

Then, on September 26, 1872, three men went to the fair being attended by thousands of people in Kansas City, Missouri. They pulled out guns, seized the cashbox containing nearly a thousand dollars in gate receipts, and dashed away. During a brief scuffle with the cashier, they fired several shots, one of which hit a small girl in the leg.

The James brothers were particularly proud of this robbery, although they could not openly admit participation in it. A letter, probably written by one of the Jameses, appeared in the Kansas City *Times* of October 15th. Signed JACK SHEPHERD, DICK TURPIN, CLAUDE DUVAL, it boasted about the robbery and proclaimed that "we rob the rich and give it to the poor." In the same paper, two days after the episode, John N. Edwards had written an editorial on "The Chivalry of Crime." It compared the outlaws with King Arthur and Sir Lancelot and described the robbery as "a feat of stupendous nerve and fearlessness that makes one's hair rise to think of it, and with a condiment of crime to season it, becomes chivalric, poetic, superb."

Major Edwards played an important role in shaping the James legend over the next dozen years. He was a diehard Rebel who, in 1865, had gone with Jo Shelby's band into Mexico rather than surrender. Reluctantly returning to Missouri, he resumed his newspaper career as editor of the *Times* and was later with the St. Louis *Dispatch*. In all of his writings, he defended the James and

Younger brothers against criticism, often supplying alibis when they were accused of robberies. Much of his argument was based upon the alleged "persecution" of former Southern men by vindictive Yankees.

Encouraged by the adulation of men like Edwards, the already egocentric Jameses continued their depredations. On May 27, 1873, four men believed to be the James gang, robbed the bank at St. Genevieve, Missouri, of $4,000. They were so self-confident that when one of their horses bolted they stopped and forced a local farmer to recover it. They also left scraps of paper behind them which said "Married Men Turn Around and Go Home. Single Men Follow."

The Jameses also began to branch out into railroad and stagecoach operations. On July 20, 1873, a Rock Island train was deliberately wrecked near Adair, Iowa. When the locomotive hit a loosened rail, it toppled over, scalding the engineer to death. The bandits lifted some $2,000 from the express-company safe in the baggage car, and then walked through the cars, taking money and jewelry from the passengers. In typical guerrilla style, they departed with rebel yells and the firing of guns.

The outlaws' swollen opinion of their own exploits was revealed by the next train robbery attributed to them, at Gad's Hill, Missouri. On January 31, 1874, five men forced the station agent to flag down the Iron Mountain Railroad's express train. They then went through the passenger and express cars, taking everything of value. As they were leaving, one of the brigands handed the conductor a "press release" containing an exact description of the holdup. It even had a headline penciled in: "THE MOST DARING TRAIN ROBBERY ON RECORD."

Jesse James also preyed on stagecoaches, though they were never as profitable as trains. On January 15, 1874, he held up the stage near the resort of Hot Springs, Arkansas. Folklore maintains that Jesse never stole from preachers, widows, or ex-Confederates. A report on this robbery in the Little Rock *Gazette* (the 18th) said that the outlaws returned a gold watch to one of the victims upon learning that he had been a Confederate soldier. However, the supposed ex-Confederate, a Mr. George Crump of Memphis, did not mention the return of the watch in his affidavit for police. It seems that Jesse kept all the jewelry. A watch and stickpin taken from Mr. John Burbank were found among the outlaw's possessions at the time of his death.

Portrait of John N. Edwards, Legend-builder. Courtesy State Historical Society of Missouri.

Jesse's profits seem to have been sizeable enough to permit marriage. In April of 1874 he wed his cousin, Zerelda Mimms. She bore him two children, Jesse Edwards James and Mary, and followed him faithfully for eight anxious years. A couple of months later, Frank James was also married, to Annie Ralston. The couple had to elope, since her father was known to disapprove of Frank and his rather dubious occupation.

In the spring of 1874, agents of the Pinkerton National Detective Agency began to appear in Missouri. They were hired from the pooled funds of railroad and express companies that were anxious to smash the James-Younger gang. But the agents were too conspicuous and too inexperienced to be effective. The Jameses were alerted to any newcomers in Clay or Jackson counties and were immediately on guard. For example, on March 11th, John Whicher adopted the "cover" of a farmer seeking work and went out to the Samuel place. The next day his bullet-riddled body was found on the road near Independence.

Pinkerton men and police were hampered by the fact that few people knew, or admitted to knowing, what Frank and Jesse James looked like. There were no photographs of them to tack up on police department walls. Various officers, such as Sheriff Boswell of Laramie City, Wyoming, were later to claim that they had arrested Jesse James but then released him since they did not know who he was. Portraits of both men were taken, but the family kept them locked up. Those acknowledged to be authentic show Jesse as about five feet ten inches tall, medium build, with sandy hair, a light beard, and icy blue eyes. He blinked excessively, a habit caused perhaps by granulated eyelids, and several reports of robberies refer to a bandit with "blinking blue eyes."

The Pinkertons made a serious blunder in their efforts to capture the two outlaws. On the night of January 26, 1875, a trainload of operatives surrounded the Samuel home on a tip that Jesse and Frank were hiding there. What was either a bomb (James family version) or an iron flare lamp filled with kerosene (Pinkerton's version) was hurled through a window, evidently to force the brothers outside. But it exploded as Mrs. Samuel attempted to shove it into the fireplace, and the fragments mangled her right arm. Arch Peyton Samuel, the nine-year-old half brother of Frank and Jesse, was killed in the blast.

There was considerable outcry against the Pinkertons, especially in the Democratic papers which tended to be somewhat sympathetic to the Jameses. Another consequence was a move to grant amnesty to the bandits. In March, a resolution to that effect was introduced in the Missouri legislature. However, it failed to get the necessary two-thirds vote, and thus was dropped. It is doubtful if the Jameses or Youngers would have surrendered had the bill passed, given their theory that old enemies were out to "get" them. Besides, they had a well-organized and successful business that yielded more money with less work than most conventional professions. Sentimentalists have said that Jesse James wanted to surrender and live a peaceful life. But all the public boasting about the brilliance of their exploits was proof that the men were incorrigible criminals, proud rather than ashamed of being outside the law.

Further proof came with the robbery of a Missouri Pacific train at Rocky Cut, near Otterville, Missouri, on July 7, 1876. Five men followed the usual technique of flagging down the locomotive and then raiding the express car, this time to the tune of $19,000. But one unusual occurrence following this holdup was the arrest of a participant! Hobbs Kerry was a young newcomer to the gang, and the lavish way he spent money in the small town of Granby right after the robbery drew the attention of detectives. After being arrested, he spilled the beans. He admitted having been on the job along with Jesse and Frank James, Cole and Bob Younger, Clell Miller, Charlie Pitts, and Bill Chadwell. However, these men were all experienced outlaws, and so attempts to apprehend them were unsuccessful.

Thus the James-Younger gang flourished in part because they operated in territory that they knew well. But Bill Chadwell (real name: Bill Stiles) was from Minnesota, and he may have suggested what turned out to be a disastrous operation. This was the attempted robbery of the First National Bank at Northfield, Minnesota, which was over four hundred miles from Clay County.

On September 7, 1876, eight men wearing linen dusters rode into town. Three of them entered the bank and ordered cashier Joseph L. Heywood to open the safe. But Heywood had backbone and refused to do so. One of the bandits, quite possibly Frank James, shot him down. The firing alerted citizens who grabbed rifles and shotguns and opened up on the outlaws. Two of the gang, Chadwell and Clell Miller, were killed in the street. The other six, several of them wounded, rode west and attempted to escape from the enrag-

ed citizens of Northfield and several other towns that were called in
on the hunt. On the 21st, a posse caught up with four of the
fugitives. In the ensuing gun battle, Charles Pitts was killed and
Cole, Bob, and Jim Younger were all captured. The two other
outlaws, Frank and Jesse James, had disappeared into Dakota Territory. They posed as law officers during their flight, telling several
citizens they were confident of catching the James Boys!

The escape of the James brothers after Northfield was a tribute to
their survivability: a key attribute of Robin Hood outlaws. Self-
preservation was maintained through an absolutely callow attitude
not only toward citizens who stood in the way but toward their own
kind as well. There are persistent traditions that Jesse James had
wanted to abandon or even finish off the badly wounded Bob
Younger since he was hindering the gang's escape. Cole of course
refused, and by staying with his brother, he was caught and
sentenced to life in the Minnesota penitentiary. If Jesse had
weakened out of some sense of loyalty to a comrade, he would have
shared the same fate — or more probably have been hanged. But he

Northfield, Minnesota as it appeared about 1870. Courtesy Minnesota
Historical Society.

was able to resist the impulse, and thus remained a free man for six more years.

Still, the James brothers were understandably nervous after the close call. They decided to take a vacation for reasons of health. For four years, from mid-1875 until October of 1879, they lived quietly in the environs of Nashville, Tennessee. Frank used the alias of "B.J. Woodson" and Jesse was "J.D. Howard." Neighbors remembered both men as being pleasant and courteous wheat speculators. Frank was more intellectually inclined than Jesse, and it is verified that he was able to quote Shakespear at length. He seems to have spent much of his time reading books, while Jesse was off at the horse races. Even though their whereabouts was unknown during those years, they continued to be the subject of rumors, and several robberies were attributed to them by various newspapers. Many of the folkloric anecdotes about Jesse James were also said to have occurred during this period. But it seems they had "got religion," more out of caution than conviction.

After three years the money ran low, and the quiet life became insufferably boring. So the two "wheat speculators" went back into the railroad business. On the night of October 8, 1879, a train of the Chicago and Alton line was held up at Glendale station about twenty miles east of Kansas City. The stationmaster was forced at gunpoint to flash the red signal. When the train stopped, the brigands stormed into the express car, knocked out the agent, and took off about $6,000 in currency. Jesse James's leadership of this robbery was later confirmed by Tucker Bassham, a gang member who turned state's evidence. He named Ed Miller, Dick Liddil, Bill Ryan, and Wood Hite as the other participants.

The resumption of outlawry became a political issue in the gubernatorial campaign of 1880. Missouri had become so notorious that newspapers across the country were calling it "The Robber State." The railroad companies wanted the outlaw gang broken up, and they backed a man whose platform included a "solemn determination to overthrow and to destroy outlawry in this state whose head and front is the James gang." The candidate was Thomas T. Crittenden, a Democrat but also a Union Man during the war. He won the election and soon afterwards persuaded the railroads to put up reward money that the state itself had been unwilling to raise.

On July 15, 1881, a Chicago and Rock Island train was robbed near Winston, sixty-five miles east of Kansas City. A half dozen men boarded the train as ordinary passengers at two different stations. Outside Winston, one of them, described as "tall and heavily bearded," suddenly stood up in the aisle and shot down the conductor, William Westfall. A passenger named McMillan panicked at this point and raced for the door, whereupon the outlaws gunned him down also. They then proceeded to rob the express car (of $10,000), stopped the train, and escaped into the night. Speculation at the time was that Westfall had been killed because he had been on the train that carried Pinkerton men to the Samuel farm before the bombing episode in 1875.

Governor Crittenden responded to the robbery by offering a reward of $5,000 each for the apprehension of Frank and Jesse James. This money was put up by the railroad and express companies, and it was tempting enough to make the brothers' lives considerably more perilous. The election of William H. Wallace as prosecutor for Jackson County also made things more difficult. Despite threats against his life, Wallace insisted on pushing the case against gang member Bill Ryan, who had been captured in Tennessee while in a drunken daze. Ryan was brought back to Jackson County and tried in connection with the Glendale robbery. He was convicted when Tucker Bassham decided to turn state's evidence and talk. A few months later, Dick Liddil surrendered and he talked. In fact, by the spring of 1882 there was a veritable Babel of voices revealing the details of every robbery by the James gang from the Liberty bank to the Winston train.

Even as the Ryan trial was about to get under way, the Jameses remained insolent. On September 7, 1881, a Chicago and Alton train was held up at Blue Cut, near the earlier Glendale robbery and right in Jackson County! The bandits found little cash in the express car, so they worked through the passenger cars extracting wallets and jewelry by means of oaths and threats of death. Various items taken in this robbery were found among Jesse James's possessions the next year, including a watch belonging to express agent, H.A. Fox.

In 1881, Jesse had moved his family from Tennessee to Kansas City. In the fall he moved again to a house in St. Joseph, Missouri, where he lived under the name of Thomas Howard. He continued to plan further robberies, and with the loss of Bassham and Ryan from the gang, he added two new men. These were Charley and Bob Ford, shifty-eyed brothers from Ray County, Missouri.

Unknown to Jesse, the two were planning to kill him for the sizeable reward, which Governor Crittenden had now upped to $10,000 for each of the Jameses. For several weeks they were in contact with the governor and Clay County Sheriff James Timberlake, discussing how best to spring the trap.

On the morning of April 3, 1882, their opportunity arrived. Jesse had taken off his pistols and was standing up on a chair to straighten a picture entitled "God Bless Our Home." Bob Ford then pulled out his revolver and sent one bullet crashing through the outlaw leader's head. Jesse was dead before he hit the floor.

Thousands of curious citizens converged on the house in St. Joseph as soon as news of the outlaw's death became known. Considerable scepticism greeted the first announcement, since newspapers had reported his "death" numerous times before. However, Zerelda James, Sheriff Timberlake, Mrs. Samuel, and others all identified the body. The coroner's examination also revealed the two scars on the chest and the clipped finger which Jesse had acquired during the war. Consequently, newspapers across the nation were soon trumpeting the news under such mocking headlines as JESSE JAMES BITES THE DUST and GOODBYE JESSE!

Not surprisingly, some of the papers denounced the manner in which he had been brought down. The editors seemed to think that shooting an unarmed man in the back was un-American. The Ford brothers were, in fact, tried for murder, found guilty, and sentenced to hang. But Governor Crittenden immediately got them released by a pardon. Just how much of the reward money they actually received remains a mystery; in any case, it did not enable them to "live happily ever after." Charley Ford committed suicide about a year later, while Bob was killed in a saloon quarrel near Creede, Colorado, in 1892.

So Jesse James died at thirty-four, a remarkably advanced age for an outlaw. In life he had almost two characters, a perfect Jekyll-and-Hyde case. At home or with trusted relatives he was a gentleman, well-groomed, careful in speech, a Bible reader, and kind to children and animals. On the job he was a brutal, cursing, remorseless killer. Jesse was smart, possibly even brilliant, but it was an intelligence severed from morality. His bloody career proves that it takes moral sense as well as brains to make a complete human being.

THE MAKING OF A HERO: 1882-1900

Jesse James was already being compared to Robin Hood in 1882, and the reference became a cliché in the years following. In its obituary story on April 4th, for example, the Kansas City *Daily Journal* said that his "shrewd, daring and desperate exploits fairly rival the deeds of Robin Hood and his merry men in England." Not everyone used the comparison as a compliment. The New York *Illustrated Times* on April 22nd said that "the savage outlaws . . . robbed and rioted in a manner for which the European freebooters of the dark ages furnish no parallel. Claude Duval, Robin Hood, and Brennan-on-the-moor, were effeminate sunflowered aesthetes compared with the Jameses and their sworn confederates." As time passed, such harsh judgments became rare, and Jesse was credited with the same virtues as the legendary English outlaw.

The component parts of such a legend had been put together years before the bandit's death. John N. Edwards played the key role of legend-builder. In his career with several Missouri newspapers during the 1870s, he was both apologist and eulogist for the James gang. In particular, he popularized two themes that were necessary to convert Jesse into a native-born heir of Robin Hood. These were the "persecution" of the Jameses by Yankees and their genuinely chivalric character and behavior.

Edwards spelled out these themes in 1877 when he published a book entitled *Noted Guerrillas, or the Warfare of the Border.* He dealt with the Jameses, Quantrill, Cole Younger, and several others whom he claimed to have known during his own career as a Confederate soldier. All these men initially became bushwhackers because of terrible wrongs done to them by Federal authorities. In Jesse's case, this was the abuse which he, his mother, and Dr. Samuel had received at the hands of militiamen in 1863. Then, after the war, "some of the ex-guerrillas were mercilessly persecuted and driven into desperate defiance." Edwards admired the way these men handled themselves after they decided upon outlawry as a way of resisting the persecutions. "They have been followed, trailed, surrounded, shot at, wounded, ambushed, surprised, watched, betrayed, proscribed, outlawed, driven from State to State, made the objective points of infallible detectives, and they have triumphed."

It was necessary to Edwards' argument that he connect the James band with the Lost Cause. So he has them saying, "we never rob Southerners." Any survey of the brothers' robberies proves this claim to be untrue, since they took wallets from Yankees and Confederates alike. Obviously, some people of pro-Southern views did sympathize with the Jameses. The gang could not have existed without the shelter and assistance given it by residents in the Kansas City-Independence-St. Joseph triangle. On the other hand, William H. Wallace, whose family supported the South during the way, maintained that "it should be stated and emphasized that the great body of the people in Missouri were opposed to the outlaw band. . . . In Clay, Jackson, Cass, Johnson, and Lafayette counties there lived a large number of ex-Guerrillas who had fought in the border warfare with the Jameses and Youngers, and who, while not approving of their depredations, were in sympathy with them on the ground of old comradeship. . . . The ex-Confederates, however, not only in the counties above-named, but throughout the state, were intensely opposed to the outlaws, and led the fight to overthrow them."

Edwards also tried to polish the characters of his heroes, rubbing away the stains to find the sterling silver underneath. So "they never boast. They speak low, are polite, deferential, and accommodating." This must have been news to any of the gang's victims. But what about the trail of corpses that Jesse and Frank had left behind them? "They do not kill save in stubborn self-defense. They have nothing in common with a murderer. They hate the highwayman and the coward. They are outlaws, but they are not criminals, no matter what prejudiced public opinion may declare, or malignant partisan dislike make noisy with reiteration." The "self-defense" theme is a familiar one in outlaw legendry, and it would be fully developed by subsequent biographers of Jesse James.

Edwards made every effort to humanize the outlaws. "They were hunted, and they were human" was one of his more memorable coinages. He removed them from the class of brutal and vicious cutpurses and executioners and made gentlemen of them. In many ways his literary operation was unsuccessful. Like a poor job of cosmetic surgery, it could not change the essential ugliness of the patient. Yet he put into print what a lot of people evidently wanted to hear about the outlaws.

The reason Major Edwards painted such an idealized portrait of the brothers was simply that he was a romantic. Familiar with English literature and mythology, he saw the James Boys as 19th century reincarnations of Sir Lancelot and Ivanhoe. Like many sensitive literary people, he found the truth painful, and could not always face it. Edwards fought a long struggle with the liquor bottle. His death in 1889 was attributed to his loss of that battle.

In 1880, two more authors made contributions to the literary exploitation of the James gang. Both books were published in St. Louis, where the writers had worked on newspapers at various times. J.A. Dacus and J.W. Buel did not share Edwards' great admiration for the outlaw brothers, and, in fact, they went in for a good deal of critical moralizing. But they both followed the essential pattern of interpretation established by the good major. The result was that both volumes added less to the historical record than they did to the evolving Robin Hood legend.

The Dacus book was published early in the year under the title *The Life and Adventures of Frank and Jesse James and the Younger Brothers.* It accepts the basic theses that persecution had driven the brothers into crime, and that they spared Southerners in their robberies. The return of Mr. Crump's watch during the Hot Springs holdup is offered as proof of the second proposition. Dacus had published books on religious subjects, and he seemed pleased that the brothers were "punctually at church sermon on Sunday." He also created some picturesque stories about Jesse's outwitting lawmen. On one occasion as possemen approached, Jesse assumed the pose and dialect of a country bumpkin: "I lives down on the Nodaway, an some infernal thief has gone off with my two best hosses. I hearn about two miles furder down at the blacksmith shop that a man passed there about an hour an a half ago with two hosses, an' they fits the descripshun of mine to a T. Have you seen sich?" Jesse then "actually turned with the two pursuers of the robbers, in pursuit of another posse of pursuers, which Jesse had been enabled accurately to describe by having seen them pass him while lying snug in a dense thicket." After riding with the manhunters for a while, Jesse gives them an excuse and slips back into the bush.

Later in the year, J.W. Buel published two paperback biographies entitled *The Border Bandits* and *The Border Outlaws.* As a reporter for the Kansas City *Daily Journal,*, he had covered several of the gang's robberies. But Buel relied as much on his imagination as he did on any factual records. He says that, as children, the brothers "manifested special delight in punishing dumb animals, which is evidenced by the cutting off of the tails and ears of dogs and cats, burying small animals alive, and diversions of every kind which would inflict the most grievous pains." This is a highly questionable interpretation, for, among other things, it is known that ten days before his death Jesse James brought home a mongrel dog for his children.

Buel pins the Russellville, Corydon, and Northfield jobs on the Jameses, but without substantiation. The speech which he has Jesse making at Corydon is amusing, but suspect: "Well, you've been having your fun and we've been having ourn. You needn't go into hysterics when I tell you that we've just been down to the bank and robbed it of every dollar in the till. If you'll go down there now you'll find the cashier tied and then if you want any of us, why, just come down and take us. Thank you for your attention."

Buel's portrait of the outlaw is a study in contradictions. Jesse is set up as a cold-blooded hooligan, but the Robin Hood theme keeps surfacing. For example, Jesse helps a destitute family in western Texas. He gets a doctor for them, prepares meals, and leaves money. On another occasion, his religiosity is demonstrated when he spares a farmer from a holdup after the farmer starts praying. When new editions of both his books were issued after Jesse's death, Buel described Bob Ford as "a traitor of the worst order, a veritable snake in the grass." This was hardly consistent with Buel's initial thesis that Jesse was a monster whom society was well rid of.

One of the most curious additions to the James biograhies was Frank Triplett's *The Life, Times, and Treacherous Death of Jesse James.* This book was published in May of 1882 as an obvious effort to capitalize on the shooting of the outlaw. Triplett says he wrote the manuscript in less than three weeks, and the book certainly shows it. He also said he had interviewed Zerelda James and Mrs. Samuel, and their signatures appear under a prefatory statement which proclaims this "the only correct and authorized edition of his life."

The *Life* is written like a Hollywood script. Jesse and Frank are cast as the unsullied heroes, while Governor Crittenden and Bob Ford play the heavies, jointly responsible for the outlaw's "treacherous" death. Triplett does not specifically develop the parallel with Robin Hood, perhaps because he views Jesse himself as "the most remarkable outlaw the world has ever seen." Some of the comparisons are implicit though, as in the justification of the outlaw's career on the grounds that the [Missouri] government was corrupt. "And what did resistance mean but a defiance of the authorities who constitute law, but alas! not always justice."

Triplett made every effort to humanize the two brothers. Neither of them is seen cutting off the ears of dumb animals. Jesse becomes something of a musician, his favorite song being "Soldier of the Cross." Frank is made out to be a student of languages, speaking French, German, and Spanish! Furthermore, Jesse is declared innocent of most robberies attributed to him, including Glendale, Winston, and Blue Cut.

While Mrs. James and Mrs. Samuel did supply some details for the book, they soon repudiated it. The reason may have been pressure from Frank James, who was still at large and who was named as a participant in several robberies, including that at Corydon. The upshot was that, although both women denied having helped Triplett, two years later they sued the publisher for a share of the royalties! The jury in the case seemed to agree that they had helped out, since it awarded them $942.

The Triplett book was only one example of how active the James family was in cashing in on the legend of their late relative. Jesse was buried on the family farm near Kearney. Mrs. Samuel charged admission to show tourists around the place and sold them pebbles from his grave. Frank James also utilized the old homestead for profit, both before and after Mrs. Samuel's death in 1911. He peddled a commercial postcard of himself standing before the house.

Incredible as it now seems, Frank James was never convicted of any crime and never served time in prison. After Jesse was killed, there were rumors that Frank was preparing to take vengeance on the Ford brothers. In fact, he was negotiating to surrender to Governor Crittenden. The intermediary was John N. Edwards, whose fine hand may be seen in the tear-inducing explanation Frank offered for his surrender:

> I was tired of an outlaw's life. I have been hunted for twenty-one years. I have literally lived in the saddle. I have never known a day of perfect peace. It was one long, anxious, inexorable, eternal vigil. When I slept it was literally in the midst of an arsenal. If I heard dogs bark more fiercely than usual, or the feet of horses in a greater volume of sound than usual, I stood

to my arms. Have you any idea of what a man must endure
who leads such a life? No, you cannot. No one can unless he
lives it for himself.

Regardless of the sincerity of this declaration, Frank did surrender
himself to Crittenden on October 5, 1882. He went through a trial
for the murder of Frank McMillan (Winston robbery), but the difficulty of obtaining witnesses and other technical flaws led to his
acquittal.

Frank James' life up until his death in 1915 certainly
demonstrated that crime doesn't always pay, for he had a difficult
time making ends meet. He held a succession of odd jobs, such as a
starter at horse races. In 1903, he appeared in a traveling circus
with Cole Younger, who had been pardoned two years before. One
of the acts featured Frank as a passenger in a stagecoach that was
held up! At the same time, he seemed to object to the competing
stage plays which were based upon the brothers' exploits. Several
stock companies toured the nation in the eighties and nineties with
melodramas such as *The James Boys in Missouri*. This drew such
crowds of men and boys at Kansas City in 1902 that Frank tried un-
successfully to get a court injunction against it. He said it painted an
overly exciting picture of outlawry and hurt his reputation as a
nonrespectable citizen. From time to time he was interviewed
about the activities of the James gang, but was understandably non-
committal. However, he did respond favorably to any stories which
cast the brothers as Good Samaritans.

The volumes by Dacus, Buel, and Triplett, along with a half
dozen other hastily written biographies, made the names and pur-
ported exploits of the James brothers familiar to millions of
Americans. Serving the same function were the hundreds of dime
novel versions of their careers. Beginning in 1881, paperback James
Boys novels tumbled from the presses of such New York publishers
as Frank Tousey and Street & Smith. Tousey's *Wide Awake Library*
included eighteen such stories between June 27, 1881, and August
22, 1883. They were all ostensibly written by "D.W. Stevens" [John
R. Musick], although other authors may have contributed. Among
the titles were *The James Boys' Longest Chase* and *The James Boys'
Cave*. Street & Smith issued many stories during the eighties and
nineties in their *Log Cabin Library*. Also, between 1901 and 1903
they had one hundred and twenty-one numbers in a series of "Jesse
James Stories." The first issues painted Jesse as a dastardly villain,

but by Number 36 he had been transformed into a do-gooder who paid off farm mortgages. Even so, parents regarded dime novels as being a bad moral influence on their children, who consequently had to bootleg the paperbacks into the house and read them surreptitiously in an attic or closet. Public pressure seems to have caused both Tousey and Street & Smith to terminate their respective James Boys series in 1903.

The one Robin Hood trait missing in the early printed accounts is that of "take from the rich and give to the poor." This idea was contributed by poor people, who have always found it appealing. Since the poor are often illiterate (and vice versa), their contribution came through folklore. Ballads and stories passed on by word of mouth were the vehicle by which Jesse James became known as a practicing socialist.

It is true that even some middle class people subscribed to the belief. Many honest citizens were hostile to the banks and railroads. During the seventies and eighties they expressed their feelings through such political parties as the Anti-Monopolists, Greenbackers, and Populists. The rail companies charged what were regarded as exorbitant rates for shipping grain to market, and when the farmer was victimized this affected storekeepers and other business people. The banks held many mortgages on which they levied high interest rates. Thus the Kansas City *Times* could say (August 23, 1876) that "the bold highwayman who does not molest the poor or the ordinary traveler, but levies tribute on banks and railroad corporations and express monopolies, is not generally such an object of popular detestation that he cannot secure a fair trial in the courts." Yet the press was usually circumscribed in its approval of banditry, both by the political power of the railroad corporations and the middle class values of its readers. The unlettered folk were under no such restrictions, and they accordingly voiced approval of the outlaws' deeds.

The ballad of "Jesse James" was the most vital statement of the belief. This ballad has dozens of versions, most of which include stanzas one and/or three below:

> Jesse James was a lad who killed many a man
> He robbed the Glendale train
> He stole from the rich and he gave to the poor,
> He'd a hand and a heart and a brain.

It was Robert Ford, that dirty little coward,
I wonder how does he feel,
For he ate of Jesse's bread and he slept in Jesse's bed,
Then he laid Jesse James in his grave.

Jesse was a man, a friend of the poor
He'd never see a man suffer pain,
And with his brother Frank he robbed the Chicago bank,
And stopped the Glendale train.

It was on a Wednesday night, the moon was shining bright,
He stopped the Glendale train,
And the people all did say for many miles away
It was robbed by Frank and Jesse James.

It was on a Saturday night, Jesse was at home,
Talking to his family brave,
Robert Ford came along like a thief in the night,
And laid Jesse James in his grave.

The people held their breath when they heard of Jesse's
death,
And wondered how he ever came to die,
It was one of the gang called little Robert Ford,
That shot Jesse James on the sly.

Jesse James went to his rest with his hand on his breast,
The devil will be upon his knee,
He was born one day in the County of Clay,
And he came from a solitary race.

This song was made by Billy Gashade,
As soon as the news did arrive,
He said there was no man with the law in his hand
Could take Jesse James when alive.

Chorus:
Jesse had a wife to mourn for his life
Three children they were brave,
But that dirty little coward that shot Mister Howard
Has laid Jesse James in his grave.

The song was probably flowing through folk channels shortly after Jesse's death, though printed versions do not appear until around 1900. It was popular with country people, black and white, in Kentucky and Tennessee, Missouri and Indiana. No one knows who composed the original ballad. The name of Billy Gashade is simply a convention, what folklorists call a "claim to authorship," rather than a factual statement. One convincing theory is that the author was a Negro convict. After all, who would be more likely to make a hero of Jesse than the poorest of the poor?

The folktale of Jesse and the Poor Widow seems to have entered oral circulation at about the same time as the ballad. The Boys meet the widow when they stop at her farmhouse for supper. During the evening she tearfully relates that she is about to lose her home to the local banker because she cannot pay the fourteen hundred dollar mortgage. Kindhearted Jesse immediately gives her the money as a gift. After she pays the debt, Jesse and Frank lie in wait and hold up the skinflint banker as he returns to town.

This episode, which appears in practically all of the printed and filmed versions of Jesse's career, has been placed in Arkansas, Tennessee, Missouri, and several other states. Although it may have blossomed from some actual episode, such as the Jameses helping the widow of a Quantrill man, it is not historically verified. It parallels the story told centuries before of Robin Hood and Sir Richard of Lee, in which the outlaw lends the nobleman money to pay church dues and then robs the Abbot of St. Mary's to recover it. The wide acceptance of this "widow" anecdote proves how readily the folk make heroes of men who seem to personify a popular concept. And not only the folk; Harry S. Truman remarked in 1949 that "Jesse James was a modern-day Robin Hood. He stole from the rich and gave to the poor, which, in general, is not a bad policy."

Folklore also deepened an idea made explicit in the biographies, and this was the gentlemanly conduct and character of the outlaws. Major Edwards' claim that the Boys were "polite, deferential, and accommodating" was mirrored in several anecdotes that make them the Protectors of Womankind. A schoolteacher on her way home with a month's wages had to go through a lonely stretch of woods. She asked a passing horseman to escort her, as she had heard Jesse James was in the neighborhood and was afraid of being robbed. The horseman took her home, and then said: "Now, lady, tell your friends that Jesse James helped you safely through the woods."

In another tale of this sort, a husband and wife were on their way to Kansas City when Jesse James robbed the train. The man slipped his wallet to his wife, but instead of demanding the money Jesse gave her a kiss!

The presumed intensity of Jesse's devotion to the Baptist religion was also cited in his favor. A common folktale that often found its way into print has it that he taught singing in the church Sunday school. This is said to have occurred on a variety of dates in several different locations, most commonly in Tennessee during the hideout years from 1876 to 1879. Unfortunately, the tradition overlooks the twin facts that Jesse was read out of the Mount Olive Baptist Church after the Gallatin robbery in 1869, and that according to his sister-in-law he could not carry a tune.

Finally, folklore made Jesse into the kind of "Clever Hero" that we expect a Robin Hood type to be. The dunderheaded officers of the law were never a match for the sharp-witted bandit. He reversed the shoes of his horses to lead them in the opposite direction. (The actual effect of such a practice would be to make the horse stumble and fall.) He posed as a country simpleton and joined a posse searching for himself (see the Dacus story above). Sitting next to an unsuspecting Pinkerton man, he tells the agent that he is in the tombstone business. On the train he meets the famous Louisville detective D.G. "Yankee" Bligh who tells "Mr. Howard" that "I'd like to see Jesse James before I die." A few days later Bligh receives a postcard which reads, "You have seen Jesse James. Now you can go ahead and die."

Even when pursuers did catch up with Jesse, folklore says they found they had caught a Tartar. A posse under Judge Alva Wycoff of Appleton City, Missouri, out with a warrant for the outlaws' arrest, suddenly found themselves surrounded and covered by the gang. After sermonizing the lawmen for a while, Jesse drove home his point by forcing Judge Wycoff to eat the warrant!

By 1900, all the essential ingredients of a Robin Hood legend had been introduced. Biography had linked Jesse James with a "cause," and had discovered redeeming traits which made him "hunted but human." Folklore had made the outlaw into a friend of the poor, and had depicted his slayer as a "dirty little coward." The printed treatments and oral traditions after 1900 consolidated these views, and in the process made the names of Robin Hood and Jesse James forever inseparable.

A TWENTIETH CENTURY LEGEND

Jesse James was one of history's liveliest corpses. He never faded from folk memory because he was being constantly resurrected, in one form or another. An example would be the appearance of men who said that Jesse has not been killed in St. Joseph, because they themselves were the one and only! Folklore spontaneously creates resurrection tales about popular outlaws, but such beliefs are usually exploited by various individuals for commercial purposes.

There were eleven major claimants to the name of Jesse James in the years after 1882, none of whom took the trouble to visit Jesse's relatives or descendants. The best known by far was the last, J. Frank Dalton. In the spring of 1948, the Lawton (Okla.) *Constitution* trumpeted his case under the banner headline, JESSE JAMES IS ALIVE! Dalton had a superficial familiarity with the details of Jesse's life and bore some physical resemblance to him. Until his death in 1951, by which time the actual Jesse James would have been 103 years old, Dalton made appearances under the outlaw's name at rodeos and state fairs. These were clearly in the nature of theatrical performances, but one man, Rudy Turilli, of Stanton, Missouri, was so positive that the old man had been Jesse James that on a national television show in 1967 he offered $10,000 to anyone who could prove otherwise. Mrs. Stella James, daughter-in-law of Jesse James, took him up on the offer. She submitted substantial historical and documentary evidence, but Turilli refused to pay her. In 1971, the courts decided that Jesse had, in fact, died in 1882, and that Mrs. James was entitled to the money.

Jesse and Frank also owed a good deal of their continued renown to the enterprise of publishing firms. For example, the I&M. Ottenheimer Company of Baltimore issued a half dozen books on the bandit brothers during the first two decades of the century. The volumes had lurid covers, sensational titles, and little new information. They did, however, buttress the Robin Hood concept. Edgar James (no relation) in *The Lives and Adventures. . .of the Notorious James Brothers,* issued in 1913, put together all the clichés in one ponderous sentence:

They were not the ordinary rough-shod highwaymen typical in the Western country, but were more of the nature of modern Robin Hoods, who robbed the rich and gave to the poor; who took human life only when they deemed it necessary for the protection of their own liberty; who were addicted to none of the ordinary vices of the bad men; who used liquor, tobacco or bad language sparingly, and who, in many particulars and traits, would have been model men had their vocations been honest and their lives unmarred by bloodshed and robbery.

After such fathers; what sons?

The standard biography appeared in 1926, and it too found an audience ready to believe the best about the outlaws. *The Rise and Fall of Jesse James* was written by a St. Louis newspaperman with the gripping name of Robertus Love. His book is probably as reliable a narrative as any "outside" investigator could have put together. It was in many ways typical of the numerous books on Western outlaws published in the years between World Wars I and II; genial in tone, romantic in outlook, and incorporating considerable folklore along with the history. Love made no bones about his admiration for the Jameses. He gave them the benefit of the doubt, and he used any colorful episodes that would make readers sympathetic with them.

An example would be the Poor Widow story, which he accepted without the flicker of an eyelash. He says this "perfect outlaw episode" reveals "a quality of mercy and justice" and "a simple human tenderness." On this and many other instances, Love practically asked his readers to stand up and applaud.

Love also used humorous dialect stories which made the outlaws appear to be more genial than they were in actuality. Following the bank robbery at St. Genevieve in 1873, the bandits forced a German-American farmer to recapture a horse for them. When the farmer did so and asked "vot do I get for dot?" Love has Jesse replying, "You get away mit your lifes, you tamned Tutchman's! Vot else you egspeck, hey, alretty yet?"

Love put into print many Missouri folk beliefs about the outlaws. People wondered why certain railroads running through the state such as the Chicago, Burlington & Quincy, were never robbed by the James gang. Love says it was because that road had given Mrs. Samuel an *annual* pass good over the entire system. This is a variant of a story appearing earlier (as in the Palmyra *Spectator* of May 8, 1890), which said that the gang spared the Hannibal & St. Joseph Railroad because it had given Mrs. Samuel a *lifetime* pass.

Love's book inspired a bushel of jocular, tongue-in-cheek articles in popular magazines. A good example would be one by Owen White and Warren Nolan in *Collier's* early in 1928. They called Jesse's birth "a real disaster," and declared that "within forty-eight hours after beginning his career, the youthful Jesse is reported to have participated in the killing of a goodly number of citizens and the looting of two nearly defenseless villages. It was a noble beginning, one that must have cheered the soul of the lad immensely." White and Nolan also commented on the folklore about the outlaw. "The numerous beds in which Jesse James slumbered and the many knives with which he ate during this portion of his career (after Pinkerton bombing) are handed down as priceless heirlooms from generation to generation." All in all, the article was a clever performance, but not one to inspire confidence.

The success of Love's book prompted motion picture companies to create their versions of Jesse's career. The outlaw, as a general type, had been a profitable subject for the movie industry since 1903, when Edwin S. Porter's *The Great Train Robbery* was made in Delaware. Only twelve minutes long, it was the first film to tell a complete story. Its basic plot of crime-pursuit-retribution has been the nucleus for virtually every outlaw picture. And Jesse James' reputation owes much to the skill with which a succession of directors and script writers have translated his legend into screen drama.

There have been some twenty-five major film versions of Jesse's career. The first important film came from Paramount in 1927. Fred Thomson, a former minister who had become a popular cowboy star of the silent era, was chosen for the lead role in *Jesse James*. A pattern was established when Thomson publicized Robin Hood concepts in interviews and press releases. He said in one interview, "never did they rob the poor and needy." Actors in all outlaw pictures have had to say publicly what they may or may not believe privately: that the character was a fine man fighting for social justice. In this picture, Jesse was depicted as the victim of Yankee persecution and made into a man without one mean trait. There are no bank or train robberies during the story, only one mild stagecoach holdup.

The classic *Jesse James* was brought out by Twentieth Century Fox in 1939. It was one of a number of "biographical films" initiated by studio head Darryl F. Zanuck. The film had everything going for

Tyrone Power as Jesse escapes from Northfield in *Jesse James* (1939). Courtesy 20th Century-Fox.

it. One of Hollywood's handsomest actors, Tyrone Power, had the lead role, and was supported by a strong cast which included Henry Fonda as Frank James. It was photographed with the new Technicolor process in the lovely countryside around Pineville, Missouri. And the script incorporated the most appealing episodes from the legend.

Scriptwriter Nunnally Johnson ignored the self-centered greed of the actual Jesse James and drew him as an idealistic social rebel. The "St. Louis Midland Railroad" persecutes the Jameses because they will not sell their land for a right of way. The company's brutish Barshee (Brian Donlevy), seemingly a composite of the Pinkerton Brothers, is the principal villain. He throws a bomb which *kills* the Boys' mother, thus providing a handy (if fictional) motive for the train robberies. "I hate the railroads," says Jesse, "they have the police, the courts, everything."

Some of the other themes handled with considerable skill were the love affair between Jesse and Zee, the relationship of the two brothers, and the subplot involving Bob Ford. The escape sequences were expertly staged. Jesse and Frank jump their horses off a cliff; they throw away money which pursuing soldiers stop to pick up; at Northfield they ride through a plate glass store window on their way out of a trap. It was such an exciting depiction that thousands of ticket-buyers must have been convinced that an outlaw's life was desirable indeed.

The script made Bob Ford a crafty, unprincipled coward. John Carradine handled the assignment so well that audiences forgot he was only playing a role. When *Jesse James* was shown in Joplin, Missouri, a man packing a revolver got up and fired six bullets into Carradine's image on the screen. Another time, when Carradine was standing in front of a theater where the film was playing, a little boy came up and kicked him in the shin.

The movie naturally took many "liberties" with history. Among the credits was one which said "Historical Materials Assembled by Jo Frances James," referring to a granddaughter of Jesse's. The studio did not, in fact, consult her during the preparation of the script. Although she finally endorsed the picture, she was as curious as anyone else about the finished product. Her comment after seeing it? "About the only connection it had with fact was that there once was a man named James and he did ride a horse."

Nevertheless, *Jesse James* was tribute to Hollywood's legend-building capacities. It established conventions that other movie-makers would copy for the next twenty years. The frequent replaying of the film on television screens during the fifties and sixties served to familiarize a vast audience with every detail of the bandit's career as seen by Darryl F. Zanuck.

If Fox's Jesse James is the classic motion picture, then Homer Croy's *Jesse James was My Neighbor* (1949) is the standard folklore collection. Croy was a fine gentleman, who had, in fact, grown up in northwest Missouri. As a schoolboy he had sung the famous ballad, explored the local "Jesse James caves," and heard every imaginable story about the celebrated outlaw. Croy *believed* in the stories he was retelling, going so far as to state that "I am not putting in this book any legends or folk tales." In fact, that is exactly what he did put in it.

All of the familiar anecdotes are here, from Jesse and the Widow to the humiliation of "Yankee" Bligh. Croy talked to residents whose families had sheltered the Jameses because "they didn't ever cause farmers any trouble. Mostly they robbed banks and railroads and express companies that had plenty of money." There were echoes of John N. Edwards in many of Croy's own statments about the outlaws. He chastised Bob Ford for taking "blood money," wagged his finger at the Pinkerton men, and dwelt at length on the attractive aspects of Jesse's and Frank's character.

Croy's was the last of the old-time sentimental interpretations of Jesse's career. In the same year that his book appeared, James Horan took a tough-minded look at the brothers' record. His *Desperate Men* was in part a history of the James gang as viewed by the Pinkerton Detective Agency, whose files he said he had used. Horan tried to demolish the favoritism-toward-Southerners and the friends-of-the-poor legends by revisionist versions of many of the gang's robberies. However, it appears he was just as predisposed to accept the Pinkertons' views of these episodes as Edwards, Love, and Croy had been to take the Jameses' side. Still, Horan did some hard digging for facts, and he opened up avenues for a debunking cycle that had been virtually dormant since 1907, when Emerson Hough had taken a brief but critical look at the Jameses in *Story of the Outlaw*.

During the sixties such professional writers as Paul Wellman, Vincent Rennert, and Dorothy Johnson followed Horan's lead in viewing the Jameses as vicious murderers. Such efforts had about as much effect on the Robin Hood legend as a dog biting the leg of a cast-iron statue. The interaction of biographical writing and folklore during three-quarters of a century had created a traditional version of Jesse's life that no amount of critical analysis could dispel.

No scholar applied his expertise to an analysis of the James story until 1966. Then William A. Settle, Jr., a professor of history, contributed a well-footnoted study entitled *Jesse James Was His Name*. The result was the definitive book on the subject, but it sold few copies in comparison with the works of Croy, Wellman, and other commercial writers. Settle too worked within the framework of the Robin Hood stereotype. For example, the name Robin Hood appears five times in the first two pages of his book, and five times in the last two pages.

Bob Ford (John Carradine) draws his gun on Jesse in *Jesse James*. Courtesy 20th Century-Fox.

One reason the revisionist's job is so difficult is that the public has not learned as much about Jesse James from historical works as they have from the various theatrical representations. Plays and movies have always done good box-office business, in part because they uniformly depict the Boys as "good badmen." This was the interpretation favored by Fox in its 1939 *Jesse James,* and by Elizabeth Beall Ginty in her 1938 stage masterpiece, *Missouri Legend.* Although a comedy, her play is a sympathetic portrait of a clean-living "Mr. Howard," who does not want the James Boys "messed up with drunkards" or with fancy women. He loves his wife, is quite religious, and has a redeeming sense of humor. He also views himself as the Robin Hood of the Ozarks. A central episode in Act Two is the gift of money to "Widow Weeks." The play has had many revivals since its first staging in New York, thus serving as another vehicle for the "traditional" version of the outlaw's character.

Numerous movie studios continued to crank out their own versions of Jesse's career. In 1950, Universal Pictures featured the World War II hero, Audie Murphy, as the outlaw in *Kansas Raiders,* acknowledged to be one of the more forgettable films on the subject. Nineteen-fifty-one saw Paramount issuing *The Great Missouri Raid.* It starred McDonald Carey, and was based on a garbled version of the legend written by Frank Gruber. For example, a railroad holdup replaces the Northfield bank es2pisode as the nearly fatal climax to the gang's early operations. An example of the characterization is that during a bank robbery, Jesse picks up a woman's purse and says, "Pardon me, ma'm, but you dropped this." Then in 1953, Robert J. Lippert produced *The Great Jesse James Raid,* with Willard Parker playing a stone-faced version of the famed brigand. The script for this one, too, had little relation to the historical background, centering on an attempt to rob a treasure of gold hidden in a mountain.

Twentieth Century Fox, possibly irritated at the amateurish efforts of its competitors, tried to repeat the success they had achieved in the Tyrone Power epic. In 1957, Fox made *The True Story of Jesse James,* with Robert Wagner playing the title role as a "misunderstood" juvenile delinquent. The research budget was increased, and a considerable effort was made to get the facts. The studio's library compiled nine fat scrapbooks jammed with information that was used to give authenticity to such background details as clothing, firearms, and railroad locomotives. Unfortunately, accuracy in physical details never guarantees reliable characterizations. The script (by Walter Newman) was somewhat more in line with history; for example, Mrs. Samuel was permitted to live beyond the bombing. But audiences did not seem to be convinced that the Jesse James portrayed was the "true" one. In addition, this film was clearly haunted by its illustrious predecessor. Action footage from the 1939 film was reused, and one could recognize Tyrone Power and Henry Fonda in some of the scenes.

It was inevitable that television would also venture into the Jesse James business. In 1965-66, the American Broadcasting Company ran a series on *The Legend of Jesse James.* The network was not sure how they wanted to portray the character, an uncertainty caused in part by a National Association of Broadcasters code which prohibited glorification of crime and criminals. Press releases stated that "the series explores the enigma that was Jesse without condoning or condemning his deeds." A young New York actor named

Christopher Jones was hired for the lead role, partly because of a physical resemblance to the outlaw. In press interviews, Allen Case, who played Frank James, gave the orthodox version of the Boys' outlawry as interpreted by Twentieth Century Fox (where the series was produced). "The railroad approached the James people and they wouldn't take the price offered, so the railroad blew up their house. As a result, the James brothers started robbing trains and giving money back to the people. That's what made them heroes."

Legend of Jesse James was dropped after only one season, the hero being killed off not by Bob Ford but by the poor Nielsen ratings. Perhaps in trying to take a neutral position on the character, the producer robbed him of all credibility. Perhaps audiences had become too knowledgeable, and could see through the falsification of history. In the thirty-minute episodes Jesse was seen killing only people worse than himself. This was carrying idealization a step too far.

In 1972, a motion picture appeared which finally did take an earthy and cynical view of the outlaws. This was Universal's *The Great Northfield, Minnesota Raid,* which featured Cliff Robertson as Cole Younger and Robert Duvall as Jesse James. The James Boys are portrayed as Bible-reading, revivalist fanatics. In their minds the Civil War is still going on in 1876, and they call the Northfield endeavor "one last guerrilla raid." Some of the familiar cinematic conventions are observed: the railroads are again blamed for the brothers' troubles, and the Poor Widow episode is included. But the brothers use profanity and tell coarse jokes. One scene shows them seated in an outdoor privy. Jesse is anything but a romantic figure; Cole Younger several times calls him "a blinky-eyed bastard." The depiction was quite a change from the sanitized Tyrone Power version, and was on that account a step in the direction of documentary reconstruction.

Similarly, United Artists' ambitious *Long Riders* in 1980 continued the cinematic de-mythologizing of the outlaw life. Jesse and Frank James, played by the actor brothers James and Stacy Keach, were seen as "good old rebels." Defeat of the Southern cause, rather than personal defects, is again the reason for their outlawry. This is exemplified when members of the gang shoot bank cashiers just because they're damn-Yankees. Jesse is steel-nerved on the job, but is a devoted family man at home. The violence associated with outlawry was realistically presented, especially in the Northfield robbery episode.

Thus the legend of Jesse James has been known in many forms to many people. It should not be overlooked that among these were other outlaws, for whom he set a standard by which they measured their own criminal accomplishments. Bob Dalton, leader of an Oklahoma gang in the 1890s, boasted that he was going "to beat anything Jesse James ever did." Such Depression-era bandits as Pretty Boy Floyd, Clyde Barrow, and Bonnie Parker were certainly familiar with his career. When Kansas City newspapers compared him with Jesse James, Floyd scrawled a reply which said "thanks for the compliments and pictures of me in your paper...Jesse James was no punk himself." Bonnie Parker fancied herself as something of a poet. One of her efforts began, "You've read the story of Jesse James — Of how he lived and died/If you're still in need of something to read, here's the story of Bonnie and Clyde." There is something uncanny about the way Jesse's reputation has shaped both action and belief for almost a century.

BILLY THE KID:
A SHORT AND VIOLENT LIFE

To some people, Billy the Kid is the perfect folk hero. They say he fought for justice and decency, took from the rich to give to the poverty-ridden, and exemplified loyalty and idealism. To others he was only a low-down horse thief and hired killer. Attempting to verify either of these views is like looking through both ends of a telescope. What is clear is that over the years a crowd of newspapermen, novelists, and script writers have seen the Kid much differently than did his contemporaries. "Posterity has been kind to Bonney," says artist Peter Hurd, "and with notable lack of evidence to merit this, the mantle of Robin Hood has descended on his narrow, bottle shoulders."

The Kid spent his childhood in several raw frontier towns. He had a succession of names — Bonney, McCarty, Antrim — that reflect his harum-scrarum personality. The place and date of his birth are unknown. Tradition has said it was New York City on November 23, 1859, but Indiana now seems just as good a bet. The Kid's mother, Catherine McCarty, is listed in the Indianapolis city directory for 1868, and it is probable that she had been living there for a number of years previously. A convincing hypothesis is that she was married to a William Bonney who became a Civil War casualty. After his death, she resumed her maiden name. Her youngest son, Henry, (Billy the Kid) carried this name in childhood and early adolescence, while the older son, Joseph, used it all his life.

Historical detectives have found that Mrs. McCarty migrated to Wichita, Kansas, about 1870. City records reveal that she purchased a vacant lot there in September of that year. In a statement accompanying the land claim, she gave her occupation as laundress, and said she had known Mr. William H. Antrim for the past six years. Antrim was a native of Indiana and had served in the state's 54th Infantry Regiment during the war. Mrs. McCarty left Wichita in the summer of 1871. She may have tarried in Denver for a while, but by the spring of 1873, she had moved with her two sons to the boom town of Silver City, New Mexico. By this time also she had married Mr. Antrim. The ceremony took place at the Presbyterian

Church in Santa Fe on March 1, 1873, with Joseph and Henry Mc-Carty being listed as witnesses.

While Antrim worked in the mines and at odd jobs, his wife made their log cabin into a boarding house. By all accounts she was a cheerful, outgoing Irish lady who worked hard. Evidently she worked much too hard. The Silver City *Mining Life* of September 19, 1874, tells us of her death from "consumption." Up to this point young Henry still had a chance in life. He had gotten enough schooling to read and to write in a fair hand. Inheriting his mother's lightheartedness, he enjoyed singing and dancing in several of the local theatrical shows. But her death when the Kid was just entering adolescence was a decisive bad break. William H. Antrim was a decent man and did the best he could for the two stepsons. The older boy, Joseph, weathered the crisis and lived to a ripe old age as a citizen of Denver. But Henry began associating with what were called "bad companions," and was to find an early grave as a hunted criminal.

The Grant County *Herald* of September 26, 1875, recorded Billy the Kid's first known crime in one memorable paragraph:

> Henry McCarty, who was arrested on Thursday and committed to the jail to await the action of the Grand Jury upon the charge of stealing clothes from Charley Sun and Sam Chung, celestials, sans cues, sans Joss sticks, escaped from prison yesterday through the chimney. It's believed that Henry was the simple tool of 'Sombrero Jack,' who done the stealing whilst Henry done the hiding. Jack has skinned out.

Henry too skipped out after climbing up the chimney. He became a drifter, a "saddle tramp," working on various ranches for board and a few dollars a month. The work was hard, the life lonely, and the temptation to relieve both boredom and poverty by a quick grab for money was ever present. Many young transients in the Southwest concluded that thievery would solve their problems, and Billy the Kid was to be among them.

In 1877, Bonney was working as a teamster at Camp Grant, Arizona Territory, when he killed his first man. It was here that he began to be called "Kid," and the nickname was not always a compliment. Bonney was a teen-ager but he always looked even younger than he was. He had a boyish face and a slight build, being about five feet eight and a hundred and forty pounds. Naturally some older and bigger men were tempted to pick on the fuzzy-cheeked youth. Frank P. Cahill, a bellowing blacksmith known as

"Windy," was one of them. He made the mistake of calling the Kid an indelicate name, whereupon the young man pulled a Colt "equalizer" and sent a bullet through his tormentor, who died the next day. The Tucson *Arizona Citizen* of August 25th reported the verdict of the coroner's inquest, which was that the shooting was "criminal and unjustifiable, and that Henry Antrim, alias Kid, is guilty thereof."

Kid Antrim was never apprehended for the Cahill shooting. Following his instincts, he departed eastward to Mesilla, perhaps planning to cross the line into Mexico if anyone should come after him. Just how he made his living in the next few months is uncertain. There is some evidence that he joined a rustling gang led by the notorious desperado Jesse Evans. The Mesilla *Independent* of October 13, reported that the gang had run off three horses, and named Henry Antrim as one of the thieves.

Sometime in the fall of 1877 the Kid rode north to Lincoln County, which then included much of eastern New Mexico. Using now the name of William Bonney, he applied for a job with John S. Chisum, the "cattle king" of the upper Pecos valley. Unsuccessful there, he appeared at the cabin of George Coe, a young homesteader who lived on the Rio Ruidoso about ten miles below the town of Lincoln. The two men became friends and spent time hunting together that fall.

George Coe and his cousin, Frank, became history's prime witnesses concerning the character of William H. Bonney. They found him to be a generally merry fellow who liked music and jokes. Physically speaking, he was nimble-footed and as graceful as a cat. When Frank played his fiddle, Bonney would dance one version of an Irish jig. The Kid sometimes pulled practical jokes that were pretty rough even by frontier standards. One time he threw a handful of live cartridges into the campfire, and then laughed heartily as the Coes jumped for cover to escape the exploding bullets. At other times they found him to be moody and evasive, never saying too much about his already troubled past. All in all, he was an unpredictable and seemingly unfathomable individual.

Through Frank Coe, the Kid was introduced to the English rancher John H. Tunstall, who hired him as a cattle hand. Tunstall was an intensely ambitious man who had come to America with a sizeable amount of investment capital, which he planned to double or triple within a few years. "I propose to confine my operations to

Billy the Kid in life. Courtesy Western History Collections, University of Oklahoma Library.

Lincoln County," he wrote his father, "but I intend to handle it in such a way as to get the half of every dollar that is made in the county by any one." Besides the ranch, Tunstall also established a general-merchandise store in Lincoln. His partner in this enterprise was Alexander A. McSween, a sharp but emotionally unstable lawyer who had come to New Mexico from Kansas, and was also seeking quick profits. John S. Chisum was involved with the two men as a silent financial partner.

The trouble with the Tunstall-McSween plans was that a powerful mercantile and ranching organization, Lawrence G. Murphy & Company, had already established itself in Lincoln County. Formed by three Civil War veterans, John H. Riley and James J. Dolan being Murphy's partners, the firm had secured juicy government supply contracts (for beef and wood) with nearby Fort Stanton. Through often questionable practices at their own store and in land deals, they had become creditors to many of the small homesteaders in the area. They had close ties with the "Santa Fe Ring," a powerful territorial political machine. In short, they were ready to fight tooth and nail against any attempt by the uppity lawyer and the fancy-pants Englishman to break up the comfortable monopoly.

Bonney scarcely got to know his employer. He was hired in December, but by February 18, 1878, Tunstall was dead. Legend was to build almost a father-son relationship out of their brief association, but this hardly seems credible. The Kid respected Tunstall alright, but loyalty for him seems to have been pretty much of a dollars-and-cents proposition. In this he was no different from the dozens of other gunmen who drifted into Lincoln County at this time, much as sharks appear in troubled waters. They hired out to whichever side offered the best deal.

Tunstall's murder was the result of an escalating rivalry between the two factions. His store offered prices lower than those of L.G. Murphy Company, and the loss of business particularly enraged James Dolan. A violent, quick-tempered man, he threatened Tunstall more than once. The Englishman underestimated the danger he was in, apparently assuming that the rule of law was as well established in the American Southwest as it was in Old England. He was, as the saying goes, dead wrong.

On February 18th, a large Murphy-Dolan posse caught Tunstall out in the open, riding along the Ruidoso. The four cowboys with him, including Billy the Kid, rode hellbent for the timber after warning their employer that he was in extreme danger. But Tunstall, proud and foolhardy to the end, reined in his horse and attempted to hold a "conversation" with the posse. They killed him on the spot.

Tunstall's death caused the outbreak of the "Lincoln County War," a complicated series of gun battles which lasted for some five months. His cowhands were henceforth employed by Alexander McSween, who also had the help of some local farmers and Mexicans. George and Frank Coe, for example, took up arms not for pay but because they had been victimized by the House of Murphy. The Mexicans either had old scores to settle, or more likely were simply pressed into service. The Murphy-Dolan-Riley forces too were the same mixture, although they probably had more hired gunmen. Some of the small ranchers joined them because they hated the land-grabbing tactics of John S. Chisum and believed that he was the real power backing Tunstall and McSween. It was unsafe for anyone to be neutral. Even Dr. Taylor Ealy, a Presbyterian medical missionary, was stopped on the street by a Murphy man who told him pointedly that he had once hanged a preacher in Arizona.

By legal maneuvering, McSween succeeded in getting warrants for the arrest of the posse that had killed Tunstall. These were issued to Dick Brewer, Tunstall's foreman. Brewer and ten more, including the Kid, caught up with two of the posse members on March 9th. Bill Morton and Frank Baker were taken captive, but were both killed "while attempting to escape." These were gang killings, since each corpse was found to have eleven bullets in it.

McSween faced two major difficulties that proved to be fatal. One was the enemy's control of the legal machinery. The physical war was accompanied by a series of political moves through which McSween tried to legitimize his grab for power. But Murphy & Company were generally successful in blocking these efforts. The territorial governor, Samuel B. Axtell, was friendly with them, so were the presumably neutral military commanders at nearby Fort Stanton. Then, too, they were able to keep their own man in the all-important office of county sheriff.

McSween's second handicap was an inability to control his own partisans. On April 1st, County Sheriff William Brady and four other men walked down Lincoln's main street on their way to the courthouse. From behind a plank gate next to the Tunstall store,

Billy the Kid and five other gunmen opened fire. Brady and deputy sheriff George Hindman were killed almost instantly. The other three dodged into a nearby store, where they fired on Bonney as he dashed out to grab Brady's new Winchester rifle. The Kid suffered a minor flesh wound in the thigh, which was treated by Dr. Ealy. McSween was angry at his men and berated them for having acted on their own. Years later, Mrs. McSween said that had her husband lived, he would have had Bonney indicted for murder. But the damage was done, and the ambush was a black mark against the McSween cause.

Later the same week, on April 4th, the Kid was present at the killing of a Murphy-Dolan gunfighter who went under the name of Andrew "Buckshot" Roberts. This episode occurred at Blazer's sawmill, several miles west of Lincoln. Dick Brewer's posse, now called "the Regulators," encountered Roberts on the porch of Blazer's home and called on him to surrender. Instead he pulled his revolver, and in the subsequent exhange of gunfire, he killed Brewer and shot off George Coe's right thumb, but was himself mortally wounded by a shot from Charley Bowdre. The Kid was named along with Bowdre and the others in an indictment for the murder of "one Roberts, against whom they had shot bullets, willfully, deliberately, and in a premeditated manner, causing his death."

There continued to be skirmishes and ambushes throughout April and May. On June 1st, Governor Axtell appointed George W. "Dad" Peppin as Lincoln County sheriff to replace the murdered Brady. In issuing his proclamation, the governor said "I urge upon all good citizens to submit to the law, remembering that violence begets violence, and that they who take the sword shall perish by the sword." The McSween men had no intention of submitting to the law when it was being administered by Murphy-Dolan adherents.

On July 15, McSween and his men rode in from the hills and attempted to seize Lincoln. When this move failed, they holed up in his fortress-like home. A party of native New Mexicans under Martin Chavez also entered town to aid McSween. Dolan and Peppin in turn marshaled their forces, who were strengthened by some two dozen fighting men from the Seven Rivers area near the Pecos.

For four days the two sides blasted away at each other with rifles. Then on the 19th, Colonel Nathan Dudley rode over from Fort Stanton with a detachment of troops, ostensibly for the purpose of protecting women and children. But he forced Martin Chavez and his men to leave town and took other actions that clearly revealed his sympathy for the Dolan faction. (A court of inquiry was later held to investigate Dudley's role in the Five-Days Battle.) That afternoon, the Dolan men managed to set fire to the west wing of the McSween house. McSween's dream of riches thus went up in smoke, and perhaps brimstone as well.

Biographers were to say that Billy the Kid directed the last defense of the house and the escape of survivors. But characteristically he was among the first to make a run for it. By nightfall the flames had consumed all the house except the kitchen, so the defenders had to make a dash for the safety of the Bonito River fifty yards aways. Alexander McSween did not make it, nor did he try. He simply stood, silhouetted by the flames, and shouted "I am McSween." Dolan's sharpshooters killed him and three other defenders. On the Murphy-Dolan side, one man, Bob Beckwith, was killed at this time. The Kid had often been named as the killer, but he was already across the Bonito when Beckwith was shot, according to the Dolan men themselves.

Thus the Lincoln County War ended, having been fought for no noble purpose. It brought only death to Tunstall and McSween; bankruptcy to the Dolan-Riley concern. Billy the Kid's role in the affair was minor. He had participated in killings (Morton-Baker and Brady-Hindman) that were essentially gangland "executions." He had also acquired a certain reputation as a desperado, which he was evidently anxious to maintain.

Bonney and other of the former "Regulators" rode up to Fort Sumner. Some of them just kept on going, out of the pages of history. The Kid, however, decided to stay in country that he knew best. As usual, he was short of money. He appealed to Mrs. McSween and to John S. Chisum for payment of what he regarded as back wages, but without success in either case. So, with half a dozen friends, he began rustling steers from Chisum's vast herds. The pretext was that if Chisum wouldn't pay them wages for their past services, they'd take it out in stock. The gang also began stealing horses, which were driven east and sold at Tascosa in the Texas Panhandle. Bonney spent the money from these transactions on card games (but little drinking) at various saloons. At Beaver Smith's establishment in Fort Sumner, he was on friendly terms with bartender Pat Garrett, six-foot-five-inch ex-buffalo hunter from Texas.

In September, 1878, General Lew Wallace replaced Samuel Axtell as New Mexico's governor, with specific instructions from the President to restore peace in Lincoln County. One of the new governor's first acts was to issue an amnesty proclamation for those who had been in the war. However, it did not apply to the Kid, who was still under indictment for the Brady assassination. A further complication was the murder of Huston I. Chapman, who was acting as Mrs. McSween's lawyer. Though Chapman was slain by a Dolan gunman, the Kid was an eyewitness to the affair, and Wallace concluded that he had somehow been involved in it. He ordered his army commander to bring in Bonney for trial and also offered a reward of $1000 for the Kid's arrest.

Wallace had taken up residence in Lincoln where he could better direct the effort to restore law and order. Much to his surprise, he received a letter from Bonney written on March 13, 1879, in which the Kid offered to surrender if the murder indictment against him could be annulled. He asserted he had been afraid to give up "because my enemies would kill me," and concluded by saying that "as to my character, I refer you to any of the citizens, for the majority of them are my friends and have been helping me all they could."

Four days later, the two men had a secret meeting at which the Kid agreed to give himself up and testify in the Chapman case. He told the governor he wanted to be kept in irons at the jail, in order to protect his reputation as a dangerous man. On the 21st, the Kid and Tom O'Folliard (also an eyewitness) did surrender and were put in the Lincoln County jail. Wallace was baffled by the popularity which such a disreputable character apparently enjoyed among the townsfolk. As he wrote to Secretary of the Interior Schurz: "A precious specimen nicknamed 'The Kid' whom the Sheriff is holding here in the Plaza, as it is called, is an object of tender regard. I heard singing and music the other night; going to the door, I found the minstrels of the village actually serenading the fellow in his prison."

In talking with Bonney later, however, the governor found him to be a shrewd observer of events in Lincoln County. The Kid was a nerveless killer all right, but he was no moron. He knew the places, the people, and the politics of the area. Perhaps as a result of this conversation Wallace began to see how bleak the prospects of reestablishing the rule of law really were. In fact, he did fail in this endeavor. His efforts were blocked by the "Santa Fe Ring," who,

Scene of Billy the Kid's exploits. Lincoln, New Mexico, as it appeared in the early 1880s. The large building in the upper center is the former Tunstall-McSween store. Building in lower left is the Murphy-Dolan store, later the county courthouse. Courtesy Special Collections, University of Arizona Library.

among other things, refused to go along with the plan of granting the Kid immunity in exchange for turning state's evidence. The Kid and O'Folliard, seeing that they had little chance of getting a pardon, easily broke what had become house arrest and headed for Roswell-on-the-Pecos. Wallace soon returned to Santa Fe where he could continue work on what seemed to be his real interest, the novel *Ben Hur*.

For the next year and a half, from the summer of 1879 to the close of 1880, the Kid headed a band of horse and cattle thieves. It operated from various hideouts in the Fort Sumner area, and included Tom O'Folliard, Charley Bowdre, Dave Rudabaugh, Billy Wilson, and Tom Pickett. Horses were stolen from ranches in New Mexico and sold in Texas; cattle were stolen in Texas and sold in New Mexico. In Arizona also there were buyers who weren't too particular about brand marks.

The big cattlemen were understandably provoked by the Kid's depredations. They may have hired a bounty hunter named Joe Grant to kill the outlaw, but if so the scheme did not work. Instead, Bonney killed Grant in a Fort Sumner saloon on January 10, 1880. The Santa Fe *New Mexican* of January 19th gave a sparse report on the episode, saying that "the origin of the difficulty was not learned." The Las Vegas (N.M.) *Optic* later added a few details under the column heading, "Kid, the Killer." "Rudolph asked Billy what had occasioned the trouble and he remarked" 'O, nothing; it was a game of two and I got there first.' The daring young rascal seemed to enjoy the telling as well as the killing."

In the middle of November, 1880, Bonney was involved in still another shooting. A posse from the town of White Oaks, forty miles north of Lincoln, trailed the gang to the ranch of Jim Greathouse. The posse's leader, a young blacksmith named Jim Carlyle, went into the house to negotiate with the outlaws, but was killed trying to get back outside. The Kid may not have fired the fatal shot, but he lost a lot of friends as a result of this episode. The Las Vegas newspapers were especially hostile. The *Gazette* of November 30th printed a scorching story about the Kid's crimes and urged lawmen to bring him to the end of a rope. Bonney was an avid reader of the papers, evidently being quite vain about his public reputation. He wrote a letter to Governor Wallace on December 12th in which he denied having killed Carlyle, and blamed his troubles on "the impression put out by Chisum and his tools."

The Carlyle affair proved what the big cattlemen had already discovered, that it was going to take dedicated professionals to break up the Kid's gang. The ranchers, therefore, hired Texas cattle detectives, and they also persuaded Pat Garrett to run for county sheriff. Garrett was ambitious, so he campaigned hard and was elected on November 7th to a job to which he was well suited. He was courageous, a good shot, and knew the country inside out. Some Bonney sympathizers accused him of being a Judas, since he had known the Kid so well during the days at Beaver Smith's saloon. But even enemies conceded his competence, and Garrett has ranked high among Western lawmen.

Garrett proved to be a patient and relentless manhunter. Both he and the Kid had friends in the area, but for a time the Kid's informants were more alert. Then on December 18th Garrett got a break when he learned that the outlaws would be visiting Fort Sumner.

He and the Texas detectives laid a trap, and when the desperadoes rode into it Tom O'Folliard was killed. The rest of the band managed to wheel about and escape. Unfortunately for them snow had fallen, so the posse was able to follow their trail to a small cabin at Stinking Springs, east of Sumner. When Charley Bowdre stepped from the cabin the next morning, he was mortally wounded in the posse's fusilade. He stumbled back inside but emerged a moment later, having been urged by Bonney to "get" one of the lawmen before he died. However, he collapsed in the snow without firing a shot. The remaining outlaws were forced to surrender. Garrett took his prisoners – Bonney, Rudabaugh, Wilson, and Picket – back to Las Vegas the day after Christmas.

The Las Vegas newspapers carried lead stories on the capture and interviews with Bonney. The reporter for the *Gazette* said that "he looked and acted a mere boy. He is about five feet eight or nine inches tall, slightly built and lithe, weighing about 140; a frank open countenance, looking like a school boy, with the traditional silky fuzz on his upper lip; clear blue eyes, with a roguish snap about them; light hair and complexion. He is, in all, quite a handsome looking fellow, the only imperfection being two prominent front teeth slightly protruding like squirrel's teeth, and he has agreeable and winning ways." Bonney seemed to treat his capture matter-of-factly, and he gave out many quotable statements: "They say 'a fool for luck and poor man for children – Garrett takes them all in.' " He again claimed to be the victim of persecution, saying that "there were certain men who wouldn't let me live in the country." He denied that he had stolen any animals, and asserted that "I wasn't the leader of any gang – I was for Billy all the time."

Bonney was held in Santa Fe for several months and then was tried in Mesilla for the murder of Sheriff Brady. With Dolan-Riley-associates like Colonel W.R. Rynerson backing the prosecution, the Kid was certain to be found guilty. He was, in fact, the only fighter in the Lincoln County War to be tried, convicted, and sentenced to death. The Kid became rather nettled at having to play the scapegoat. The Las Vegas *Gazette* of April 5, 1881, quoted him as saying that at least two hundred men had been killed in Lincoln County during the past three years, and that he did not kill all of them. Still, he maintained his usual phlegmatic attitude. The court clerk, I.M. Bond, remembered that the Kid "took no more interest in the trial than I would in a hand organ and a monkey."

Bonney was taken to the Lincoln County courthouse (the old Murphy-Dolan store) to await hanging on May 13. On Thursday, April 28, while Garrett was out collecting taxes, the Kid escaped after shooting his two guards, J.W. Bell and Bob Olinger. Just how the escape was engineered is not known, but it probably involved outside help. One theory is that friends of the Kid hid a six-shooter in the privy in back of the courthouse. Billy got the drop on Bell, but had to shoot when Bell tried to break away. The Kid then grabbed Olinger's loaded shotgun from the armory. When Olinger approached the courthouse from a restaurant across the street, the Kid greeted him from the second floor window and then gunned him down. "After killing Bell and Olinger," reported the Las Vegas *Optic*, "Kid compelled Mr. Goss to saddle Mr. Wm. Burt's horse for him, and rode quietly and leisurely out of town, no one offering to molest him in any way." The citizens' failure to try and stop the Kid may not have been admirable, but it was certainly wise.

The territory's newspapers uniformly deplored the Kid's escape, and condemned him in no uncertain terms. The *Optic* of May 4 said that "with a character possessing the attributes of the damned, he has reveled in brutal murder and gloried in his shame. He has broken more loving hearts and filled more untimely graves than he has lived years, and that he is again turned loose like some devouring beast upon the public is cause at once for consternation and regret." Conversely, the two dead lawmen were eulogized, the White Oaks *Golden Era* of May 5 saying that Olinger "was admired for his efficiency as an officer and his bravery and geniality as a man."

After his escape, the Kid hid out in the Fort Sumner area. He enjoyed the hospitality of sheep camps, and some newspaper reports said he had stained his skin to look like a native herder. Why he did not take the opportunity to escape into Old Mexico is one of the great puzzles in his biography. Maybe it was just a case of habit overpowering common sense. Local gossip said it was because he had a girlfriend at Sumner, but the Kid's consistency in looking out for himself first of all, casts doubt on this theory. At any rate, by hovering around the familiar haunts, he doubled the chances of being caught.

Pat Garrett finally killed the Kid on July 14, 1881. That evening, he decided to follow up a tip that the fugitive was staying with Pete Maxwell, a sheep rancher who had a house on the grounds of the old fort. Garrett went out to Maxwell's place accompanied by deputies John W. Poe and Thomas T. McKinney. He entered the rancher's bedroom and had been conversing with him for only a few moments when a man in stocking feet and carrying a butcher knife appeared in the doorway. Unable to see in the dark, the man called out *"Quien es?" "Quien es?"* [Who is it?] Garrett, recognizing the voice, pulled his revolver and fired two shots, the first of which caught Bonney right through the heart.

The newspapers were overjoyed to hear about the outlaw's demise. Even in the Kid's hometown of Silver City, the *New Southwest* and *Grant County Herald,* in their obituary stories on July 23, exulted that "the vulgar murderer and desperado known as 'Billy the Kid' has met his just deserts at last...the fact is he was a lowdown vulgar cutthroat, with probably not one redeeming quality." The papers also gave Pat Garrett well-deserved credit for having done a dangerous job. John W. Poe was later to say that the Kid's death was "foreordained...by a Higher Power." That may be, but Garrett surely gave the Power a helping hand.

10

A MAN "ALL BAD"

Billy the Kid became a nationally-known figure at the time of his death, although he was regarded as anything but another Robin Hood. The American News Company, a commercial service, prepared a brief story of his career which was widely reprinted. Even the far-off *London Times* (August 18, 1881) thought it was worth using. The papers in Kansas City, Chicago, Philadelphia, and New York carried more or less elaborate biographical summaries, which were often padded with speculation. They asserted, for example, that Bonney was twenty-one years old, and then with an eye for mathematical symmetry concluded that he had killed twenty-one men! The editors evidently admired the desperado's coolness, but generally they followed the territorial papers in viewing him as a bloodthirsty monster in human form.

The *National Police Gazette* and the dime novelists quickly exploited the sensational possibilities of the Kid's career. On May 21, 1881, the *Gazette* had carried a story on "Billy the Kid's Exploit," which described his escape from Lincoln. That summer the *Gazette's* publisher, Richard K. Fox, issued Thomas F. Daggett's *The Life and Deeds of Billy Leroy, alias The Kid, King of American Highwaymen.* Although the bandit is called "Leroy," the story deals with the Lincoln County War and events in the life of Billy Bonney.

Garbled versions of the War were also incorporated in the dozen or so dime novels about the Kid. Two of these are both entitled *The True Life of Billy the Kid.* The first one was by Don Jenardo [John Woodruff Lewis], and was issued on August 29, 1881, as number 451 in Frank Tousey's "Wide Awake Library." Lewis depicts Bonney as a smirking psychopath. After each murder, the Kid gives "the laugh of a demon," or "the grin of a devil." He is made a ravisher of women, and is the tool of his worthless employers Chisum and "McSwain." "How many murders he committed, how many cattle he stole, how many daring deeds of deviltry he performed, will never be known until the dark deeds of cowboys, congressmen, governors, thieves, law-makers, law-breakers, are laid bare to the world."

The second *True Life* was issued in September by the Denver Publishing Company, and is credited to the aptly named Edmund

Fable, Jr. This author is slightly kinder to Bonney. At least the outlaw's career originates in some outside provocation, rather than in his own twisted personality. In Silver City he is unjustly thrown in jail on a trumped-up robbery charge. He escapes and fights for the Englishman "Tonstill" in the range war. The Kid establishes headquarters in an adobe castle on the Staked Plains where he struts around dressed like a peacock: blue dragoon's jacket, black buckskin pants trimmed with silver bells, and a beaver hat covered with jewels.

Much of this fanciful material did not originate in Fable's whiskied brain, but was borrowed from the more outrageous newspaper reports. The assertion that the Kid had shot twenty-one men, which seems to have been made first by the Santa Fe *Weekly Democrat* for July 21, 1881, was the favorite legend. Another unfounded story was that of the Kid's riding into one of John Chisum's camps and shooting three of the four cowboys there, as "payment" for back wages. This tale was first printed in the Santa Fe *New Mexican* of May 1st, 1881. The Las Vegas *Optic* of June 10th picked it up, and though the rival Las Vegas *Gazette* (June 16th) denounced the report as "entirely false and without foundation," it had already become embedded in the legend. Thus Fable in his novel gave wider circulation to the commonly held view that the Kid was a wanton killer.

The initial newspaper stories and dime novels were sterile ground as far as any Robin Hood legend was concerned. Enter Pat Garrett and M. Ashmun Upson, who collaborated on a published biography that made the germination of such a legend possible. The book appeared in April of 1882 under the title *The Authentic Life of Billy, the Kid.*

The motives of the two authors practically guaranteed some build-up of the Kid's reputation. Garrett was politically ambitious, so he was hardly going to say that the outlaw he'd killed at Fort Sumner was an insignificant punk. Instead, Bonney becomes "the peer of any fabled brigand on record, unequalled in desperate courage, presence of mind in danger, devotion to his allies, generosity to his foes, gallantry, and all the elements which appeal to the holier emotions." That the Kid was "generous to his foes" must have been startling news indeed to the survivors in Lincoln County! Robin Hood is not mentioned in Garrett's introduction paean, but Dick Turpin and Claude Duval are named as comparable outlaws.

Ash Upson ghosted the biography to make money rather than to record history. Although primarily an itinerant newspaperman, he had also worked as a storekeeper, surveyor, and postmaster to make ends meet. A jovial old soul, he was like so many frontier journalists in that he had great trouble remaining sober. His major task was to make the *Life* so appealing that it would get the same kind of mass readership that the dime novels enjoyed. Hence he sensationalized and to an extent fictionalized the Kid's life to achieve saleability.

Upson has the Kid killing his first man in Silver City when he was only twelve years old. An unnamed "filthy loafer" insults the Kid's mother on the street. Later this same loafer attacks the boy's adult friend, Ed Moulton, in a saloon, and so the youngster pulls a knife and stabs him. This imaginative story had been going the rounds long before Upson immortalized it in print. The *New Southwest and Grant County Herald* of July 23, 1881, remarked that "the story that he killed 'his first man' for insulting his mother is a fabrication." Another one who branded the story a lie was none other than Ed Moulton! Upson knew, however, that in Victorian America an insult-to-motherhood episode would be a sure-fire way of creating sympathy for his hero, so he put one in.

There are other generous acts which help redeem the Kid's crimes, and which take his characterization a step closer to the Robin Hood ideal. He and another "young knight," Jesse Evans no less, rescue a wagon train from the Apaches. The Kid uses an axe to dispatch eight of the redskins. Bonney also rides eighty-one miles in six hours to rescue an old comrade, Melquiades Segura, from a jail in San Elizario, Texas. This was certainly a long ride – and an equally tall tale.

Neither Garrett nor Upson had taken part in the Lincoln County War, yet they boldly credit the Kid with most of the killings by the McSween faction. They report twelve victims of his guns, a three-fold exaggeration as subsequent researchers were to discover. Upson declared that these killings were revenge for the assassination of Tunstall, for whom the Kid entertained "a strong friendship and deep respect, which was fully reciprocated by Tunstall." This supposition of a father-son relationship was thus welded into the legend.

The *Authentic Life* was a disappointment to the co-authors because it did not sell well. In a letter to a relative, Upson blamed the publisher, the Santa Fe *New Mexican,* for a poor marketing job. It seems more likely that public opinion was not yet prepared to accept Bonney as the kind of knight errant that the authors tried to make of him. Local reaction to the volume was decidely cool. The Las Vegas *Gazette* (October 22, 1881) reported a comment from the Mora *Pioneer* which questioned Garrett's motives: "We can see no pressing necessity for the work he is to have printed, and can only look on it as the means of reaping a further harvest from a lucky shot." Yet the book added substantially to the legend, since it publicized the Kid's name and became the principal source used by subsequent biographers.

Charles Siringo also viewed the Kid more sympathetically than most contemporaries in his book, *A Texas Cowboy,* published in 1885. His sentimental attitude is remarkable in that the Southwestern cowboys had no use for Billy the Kid. One searches in vain among their traditions for any ballads, tales or other oral legends about the desperado. He was after all a thief, whereas the cowboys were committed to a code which centered on protection of their employer's property at all costs. Such men would have little use for a rustler who looked to his own selfish interests above all else.

As a cattle detective in 1880, Siringo had participated in the effort to break up the Kid's gang. He devoted a chapter of his tome to a sketch of the outlaw, asserting that "the Kid was not the cruelhearted wretch that he was pictured out to be in scores of yellow-back novels written about him. He was an outlaw and may be a very wicked youth, but then he had some good qualities which, now that he is no more, he should be credited with." Among other things, the kid is generous, compassionate, and capable of affection. Good Samaritan that he is, he cares for a (unidentified) sick man and pays the fellow's bills. Siringo also smoothed the sharp edges of the Kid's personality by hinting at romantic attachments: "the remains of what was once a fond mother's darling were buried next day in the old dilapidated Military Cemetery, without a murmur, except from one, a pretty young half-breed Mexican damsel, whose tears, no doubt, had dampened the lonely grave more than once."

Bonney was in fact regarded as something of a cow country Romeo. He had a boyish charm, was a fair dancer, and dressed carefully for social occasions. Sallie Chisum Roberts, Mrs. Susan

McSween, and other women of the time remembered him as an engaging young man. The Kid certainly had girlfriends in the Mexican community. Various names were mentioned, including that of a married woman, Celsa Gutierrez. In later editions of his very popular book (which he claimed had sold a million copies during his life), Siringo called the lady Dulcinea del Toboso, a code name drawn from the novel *Don Quixote*.

The presumption that the Kid was a hero to the Spanish-speaking people became an essential component of his legend. The belief is based first of all on the fact that he did have Mexican girlfriends, and second upon the testimony of several Mexicans who fought for the McSween side in the Lincoln County War. A good example of the latter would be Ygenio Salazar, who had been only fifteen years old in 1878 when he was called out to help defend the McSween house. He was hit by four bullets and fell unconscious, escaping only because the Murphy-Dolan men thought he was dead. Salazar spoke freely to numerous interviewers until he passed away in 1936, and he always praised the Kid as a likeable fellow who had been grossly wronged. Mexicans who had fought for Murphy and Dolan, on the other hand, were never interviewed by reporters or biographers.

Actually, the Kid's welcome reception may be explained by the old Spanish "honor code," which obligates one to help strangers. This is a special responsibility if guests are the weak, the "underdogs," and the Kid was probably seen in this role after the defeat of the McSween party. For his part, the Kid probably sought refuge with the Mexicans for purely opportunistic reasons. It was safer to stay in the little adobe *casas* or at the sheep camps than in places like Lincoln or Fort Sumner. He was sure of being fed and was pretty well sheltered from the prying eyes of Sheriff Garrett or the cattle detectives.

On the other hand, Garrett too had the support of many Spanish-speaking people, in part because of his marriage to Polinaria Gutierrez. It should also be noted that the verdict of the inquest into Bonney's death, which stated that "we are united in the opinion that the gratitude of all the community is due said Garrett for his action," was signed by five Spanish-Americans.

What Spanish-language folklore there is about the Kid also makes it doubtful that he was regarded as a hero. The topical folk song (*corrido*) entitled *Campana de los Bilitos* lionizes not the Kid but Pat

Garrett, "the man to whom we owe this great deed [killing the Kid] we will never forget." *Muerte del Afamado Bilito* says he committed such foul crimes that his death was welcomed; *"su muerte fue aplaudida."* This ballad also refers to the Kid's "criminal smile" and his "cruel and bitter hand" – hardly the language of hero worship.

The same attitudes appear in what is apparently the first "Billy the Kid" ballad in English. Collected by John Lomax in 1911 from a singer near Tucson, Arizona, it begins: "Billy was a bad man and carried a big gun/he was always after Greasers and kept 'em on the run." The short text goes on with some more unflattering comments about the outlaw's crimes, and concludes, "now he's dead, and we ain't none the sadder." This ballad never flourished in oral tradition, but it reveals a view that must have been shared by many Southwesterners.

For almost a half century after the outlaw's demise, most people still viewed him an an arch-fiend. Emerson Hough was one of the writers who kept this idea before the public. Hough had been a lawyer at White Oaks in 1883 and had subsequently done professional writing as a sideline. His *Story of the Cowboy* (1897) included material on the Kid which was derived from gossip he had heard around the town, whose citizens were bitter about the outlaw because of the Carlyle shooting. Hough calls the Kid "the notorious cut-throat." He also denies that Bonney was a hero to the Mexicans. Instead, he has the outlaw and his gang shooting down seven Mexicans "just to see them kick." This story seems to have grown from the coincidence that one Charlie Wall was in the Lincoln jail at the same time as the Kid, on a charge of having killed four Mexicans during a dispute over water rights. By simple transference, this episode was tacked onto the Kid's record by Hough and other writers who wanted to demonstrate how cold-blooded he really was.

Another variation on the same theme was Arthur Chapman's article for *Outing Magazine* in 1905 entitled "Billy the Kid – A Man All 'Bad.'" Again the Kid guns down those Mexicans "just to see them kick." In the Lincoln County War he serves the "rustlers" rather than the upstanding citizens. Chapman's most imaginative story concerns the Kid's trial at Mesilla. Judge Warren Bristol sentences the outlaw "to be hanged by the neck until you are dead, dead, dead. . . . Whereupon the boyish prisoner laughed in the judge's face and chanted in mockery, 'And you can go to h-l, h-l, h-l!'" This story, reprinted many times over the years, makes Bonney into an insolent punk.

After Chapman's article, there was little interest in the Bonney legend until the mid-1920s. Several magazine pieces and a few biographical sketches in books on Western history were only faint reminders that Billy the Kid had ever existed. He was fading into obscurity, no more worthy of being remembered than such contemporaries as "the Pock-Marked Kid" or "Saw Dust Charlie." Authors had done such a thorough job of depicting the outlaw as a "Man All Bad" that they nearly extinguished the embers that were to flame up into a Robin Hood legend with the passage of time.

MR. BONNEY AND THE FAKING OF HISTORY

In 1925, the remodeling of the Bonney legend began in earnest. Harvey Fergusson, who came from a distinguished New Mexico literary family, put his talents to work on a magazine article that described the Kid as a romantic and an idealist. This more favorable view of the outlaw did not result from a discovery of any new historical evidence, but simply the passing of the years. It was a case of a legend whose time had come. The middle class readers of the then-influential *American Mercury* were evidently ready for Fergusson's portrait of a selfless youth who became the victim of fate.

Fergusson based his sketch on the Garrett-Upson biography and Charlie Siringo's book. He repeated such Garrett-Upson stories as the stabbing of the "loafer" at Silver City and the rescue of a wagon train from Apaches, since they highlighted the Kid's idealism. Readers further learned that when he fought in the Lincoln County Wars, Bonney was "a quixotic romantic, who cared nothing for money" – a shocking revelation if only it were true. The Kid's romantic nature also explains his death, since he simply could not leave his Mexican *querida* at Fort Sumner. Finally, Ferguson linked Bonney with the indispensible social-justice theme: "Like Robin Hood, he befriended the poor."

Fergusson's effort was followed within a year by the *magnum opus* of the Bonney legend. This was Walter Noble Burns's *Saga of Billy the Kid,* a book so cleverly structured and written that it became the fountainhead from which gushed a torrent of ballads, movies, and imitative biographies. Early in the book Burns declared that the Kid was "destined eventually to be transformed by popular legend into the Robin Hood of New Mexico," a self-fulfilling prophecy since Burns himself proceeded to do the transforming.

The author was a Chicago newspaperman who went to Lincoln County and interviewed old-timers. Unfortunately, he talked only with McSween partisans and Bonney sympathizers. Had he sought some contrary opinions, the *Saga* might have been a balanced historical account. Instead, it was an idealized portrait of an outlaw who emerged as larger than life and a one-sided tribute to the "lost cause" of McSween and Tunstall.

Burns heard from such people as Frank and George Coe, Ygenio Salazar, and Mrs. Jose Jaramillo. All were effusive in their praise of the Kid. Frank Coe said he'd been a generous boy who would "give a friend the shirt off his back." Mrs. Jaramillo said "he was a nice boy, at least to me, courteous, gallant, always respectful." No wonder Burns became convinced that the Kid was an idealist. Echoing Ferguson, he declared that "others fought for hire. Billy the Kid's inspiration was the loyalty of friendship." Such views are incredibly naive, given the Kid's record and his own admission that "I was for Billy all the time."

If the Kid were such a nice fellow, those who had opposed him must necessarily have been nasty people. This thinking might have been valid for certain members of the Murphy-Dolan combine, but it resulted in unduly harsh portraits of Pat Garrett and Bob Olinger. Garrett is a Judas because he hunts down his one-time friend. Inferences of unfairness punctuate Burn's description of Garrett's effort to break up the Kid's rustling gang. Manipulation of chronology (Burns cites only three dates in the book) serves to create sympathy for the outlaws and to make Garrett appear as an unfeeling mercenary. For example, when the gang rides into Fort Sumner on Christmas Eve, the sheriff violates the holiday spirit by firing on them and killing off Tom O'Folliard. The trouble here is that this heartrending scene occurred on December 18th.

Bob Olinger becomes a bully who taunts the Kid unmercifully during his incarceration at Lincoln. "He never ceased to revile the Kid in tirades of scurrility and billingsgate." Contemporary sources, however, describe Olinger as a worthy peace officer who treated prisoners fairly enough. Lily Klasner, for example, knew him as a resolute but quiet man, not the type to torment and taunt people. It seems that if Billy the Kid is to be a hero, then Olinger has to be the conventional villain even if this requires a distortion of his character.

To transform Bonney into a Robin Hood, Burns had to find stories which centered on such appropriate traits as generosity, cleverness, and concern for the poor. He therefore pretended that he had found "innumerable stories" in both the Anglo and Mexican communities: "they are told at every campfire on the range; they enliven the winter evenings in every Mexican home." But no examples are given, and the "tale-tellers" are composite characters rather than specific individuals. The truth was that the Kid was never a folk hero, but nevertheless Burns's literary kiss turned the frog into a prince.

Burns credited the Kid with many clever exploits. One of the most puzzling episodes in the Kid's biography is just how he managed to kill Joe Grant at Fort Sumner. According to Burns, he admired Grant's gun, asked to examine it, and while doing so set the hammer on an empty chamber. Then when Grant drew on the Kid he was easily dispatched. Contemporary reports do not say how the Kid killed the Texan. Burns just used his imagination to make the Kid look good.

Finally, Burns employed a you-are-there technique with reams of dialogue. Historians usually regard the use of dialogue as suitable only in works of fiction. There are no records of what people actually said on the numerous occasions where Burns purports to give their exact words: the "last stand" at the McSween house; the Joe Grant shooting; the Kid's final conversation with Celsa Gutierrez at Maxwell's place. Furthermore, it is hard to believe that Burns really knew what his cool hero was doing during the siege of the house; "A Murphy bullet knocked a cigarette from between his lips. 'Now that's too bad,' he said cheerfully, 'I'll have to roll another.'"How did the author know that as the Kid raced from the burning house, "his foes fired more than fifty shots at him"? Burns was so carried away by his own enthusiasm that he saw the Kid as superhuman; "not a bullet touched his body. On he ran like a darting, elusive shadow as if under mystic protection." Such magical escapes belong to figures of fiction and folklore rather than to those in real life. All in all, the *Saga* has the earmarks of a novel rather than a biography.

Perhaps because of its literary virtuosity, the book became the most influential volume on "the idol of the Southwest." It was well received on publication, and was chosen for the Book-of-the-Month Club. It revived the Bonney legend by painting the canvas in bold strokes and bright colors that everyone could understand.

The most immediate result of Burns's *chef d'oeuvre* was the manufacture of other so-called "folk" traditions. In 1927 a ballad of "Billie the Kid" was composed by the Reverend Andrew Jenkins, who had received a copy of the *Saga* from a music agent. The text repeated many of the familiar legends about the outlaw:

> I'll sing you a true song of Billie the Kid,
> I'll sing of the desperate deeds that he did;
> Way out in New Mexico long, long ago
> When a man's only chance was an old forty-four.

When Billie the Kid was a very young lad
Out in Silver City he went to the bad;
Way out in the West with a gun in his hand —
Altho but twelve years old, he killed his first man.

Fair Mexican Maidens play guitars and sing
A song about Billie their boy-bandit king;
How ere his young manhood had reached its sad end
Had a notch on his pistol for twenty-one men.

On the very same night when poor Billie had died —
He said to his friends, I am not satisfied
There were twenty-one men I have put bullets through
And Sheriff Pat Garrett must make twenty-two.

Now this is how Billie the Kid met his fate,
The bright moon was shining, the hour was late —
Shot down by Pat Garrett who once was his friend,
The young outlaw's life had now come to its end.

Down in Pecos Valley all covered with green
Out in "Hell's Half-acre" three graves can be seen;
Where Tommie and Charlie and Billie now lie,
Their trail of blood ended, they all had to die.

There's many a young man with face fine and fair
Who starts out in life with a chance to be square;
But just like poor Billie, he wanders astray,
And loses his life in the very same way.

This relatively late addition to the legend did not become really well known until record companies began issuing commercial versions of it. Early in 1927, RCA Victor brought out "Billie the Kid" sung by Vernon Dalhart. Woody Guthrie became the most influential artist to popularize the ballad when he recorded it in the 1930s, although he revised the Jenkins text so extensively that it became almost another version. Most people who hear this song assume that it dates from the cow camps of the 1880s.

A rash of newspaper and magazine stories about the outlaw also appeared in the wake of Burns's book. "Resurrection" tales were quite popular for a while. Like Lazarus risen from the dead, the Kid was alive and well and living on an isolated ranch in New Mexico, or was a prosperous businessman in Texas, or was farming down in Old Mexico. The El Paso *Times* of June 29, 1926, carried a report that he was "living within 200 miles of the city." The gist of the fairy tale was that Garrett had collaborated with the Kid in passing off the corpse of some nobody as the Kid's. As late as 1940, the WPA-sponsored *New Mexico: A Guide to the Colorful State* was reporting that "a number of people in remote parts of the state believe the Kid is still alive, despite the fact that the circumstances of his death are well authenticated."

Inevitably there appeared an individual who claimed that he was Billy the Kid. This was one "Brushy Bill" Roberts, who in 1950 emerged from obscurity to ask the governor of New Mexico for a pardon. A few years later a book was published that tried to validate Roberts' claim, but by that time even the most misty-eyed romantics were ready to concede that Bonney was pushing up daisies.

Walter Noble Burns had been the first writer to popularize the idea that the Kid was a hero to the Mexican-Americans. The idea was conveyed by imagery rather than by concrete evidence. Strumming guitars, steaming bowls of chile, and gaily bedecked senoritas are some of the props that Burns employed quite effectively. So it wasn't long before other tales of the Kid's magnanimity to this group began to appear. Frank Applegate, for example, collected a story in which Bonney saves a girl from the unwelcome attentions of the "bad" outlaw Ruiz. Interviews with Mexican families for the Federal Writers Project, although not published, yielded the same type of anecdote. Only rarely do the statements seem to reflect folk memory; more often they merely echo Burns's phrases.

The foremost statement of this particular theme came with the publication of Miguel A. Otero's *The Real Billy the Kid,* in 1936. Otero had talked briefly with the Kid at the Las Vegas jail in 1880. His career in New Mexico politics had included the governorship (1897-1906). In his book, Otero said that the Kid "had a reputation for being considerate of the old, the young, and the poor; he was loyal to his friends and, above all, loved his mother devotedly. He was unfortunate in starting life, and became a victim of circumstance." Interviews with other Mexicanos buttressed this extremely favorable interpretation. Ygenio Salazar said that the outlaw "was kind and good to poor people, and he was always a gentleman, no matter where he was." Martin Chavez reported that "Billy was one of the kindest and best boys I ever knew, and far superior in many respects to his pursuers. He was not bloodthirsty, he was forced into killing in defense of his own life."

So the Kid's hero status among the Mexicanos became another cliché, even though the evidence is contradictory and inconclusive. Many Anglo-Americans accepted the legend at face value, and seemed to feel that Bonney should be condemned not simply because he had been a thief, but because he had been too darned friendly with the natives. Mrs. Sophie Poe, wife of Garrett's deputy, maintained that he was "good to Mexicans. He was like Robin Hood; he'd steal from the white people and give it to the Mexicans, so they thought he was all right."

The theme was to be expressed in even the most exotic art forms. Aaron Copland created a "character-ballet," full of symbolism, in which the Mexican sweetheart and a chorus of mourning women play central roles. Copland's *Billy the Kid* was first performed at the Chicago Civic Opera House during November of 1938, and has been frequently restaged ever since. That the nimble-footed cow thief of the 1880s should be reincarnated years later in the person of a graceful ballet dancer performing for sophisticated audiences seems quite appropriate to the legend.

Burns's *Saga* was written so much like a movie script that it was no surprise when Metro-Goldwyn-Mayer purchased the film rights. Director King Vidor was able to convince the studio heads that audiences were ready for "honest brutality." So *Billy the Kid* was released in 1930. It starred Johnny Mack Brown, who had been an All-American football player at the University of Alabama. He handled the role with athletic verve and a pronounced Southern accent.

The Kid was depicted as a philanthropic type who shoots only to avenge wrongs done to friends. As his sweetheart "Miss Claire" tells him: "Every killing you've done was needed." A preface by Governor C.M. Dillon of New Mexico said that although the movie "took liberties with history," it was a "true drama" of the now-famous outlaw. Among the "liberties" was the role assigned to Pat Garrett, played with avuncular charm by Wallace Beery. The Sheriff is active on the Murphy-Dolan side and indeed directs the final assault on the McSween house. Also, the Kid was permitted to escape to Old Mexico with Miss Claire at the end of the story. The sentimental character portrayals were balanced somewhat by the stark and dusty landscapes of the Grand Canyon and Zion Canyon, where the picture was photographed.

MGM found the outlaw such a profitable subject that in 1941 it produced another *Billy the Kid*. This one starred Robert Taylor, with Brian Donlevy cast as "Sheriff Jim Sherwood." Taylor appeared too dignified and gentlemanly to make a convincing desperado. The most laughable scene was that of the final shootout. The Kid is so fond of his former friend that, instead of drawing his gun with the right hand, he uses the left, thus allowing the slow-drawing sheriff to drill him full of holes! *Life Magazine* was fully justified in titling its review-article "Billy the Kid: in Two Films about Him Hollywood Fakes History."

The other picture reviewed in the article was not actually released until 1943. This was *The Outlaw,* personally produced by Howard Hughes and featuring Jack Beutel as the Kid and Jane Russell as his girlfriend, "Rio." The film attempted to exploit the erotic aspects of the Kid's life, and this brought on a long struggle with censors who demanded the cutting of certain scenes. Hughes designed a special "heaving" brassiere which focused the audience's attention on Miss Russell's ample bosoms — at the expense of the story line. *The Outlaw* was actually a quite realistic film biography, but because of its distribution problems it has little effect on the legend.

Billy the Kid in legend. Brian Donlevy and Robert Taylor in a scene from *Billy the Kid* (1941). Courtesy Metro-Goldwyn-Mayer.

The unidentified *Life* reviewer also made an accurate assessment of the Kid's status as of 1941. "Today he has assumed the lofty position of a U.S. Robin Hood, a Southwest symbol of fearless, romantic youth." Indeed, Walter Noble Burns had triggered a fifteen-year boom in books, ballads, and films whose effect was to make the Bonney legend an inseparable part of the national culture. The Kid's Robin Hood status continued to be the premise of many novels, biographies, and movies, although there were also notable variations from the norm.

Edwin Corle, for example, was one novelist who saw the Kid as a steely-eyed executioner. Corle made extensive claims for the historical validity of his *Billy the Kid,* published in 1953. In an "Author to Reader" note, he says that the novel "contains many historical truths; I believe that it tells the story of Billy with veracity." Among the revelations are scenes of the Kid's birth in New York City, the details of his first crime (the knife-murder of a Chinese laundryman in Silver City), the true story of his only love affair, and the latest explanation of how he got the gun that enabled him to escape from Lincoln jail. The love affair is with a married woman, Abrana Garcia. The Kid is so infatuated with her that he is willing to kill off the husband should he stand in the way. Bonney emerges as quite an unattractive figure, a man with "subzero emotions." Corle follows Burns in viewing the Kid as a leader of men, who had a charmed life. But these qualities do not redeem his selfish and conscienceless personality. Significantly the Mexican-Americans, who are indispensible to the Robin Hood concept, are practically ignored until the last two chapters.

Charles Neider in his *Authentic Death of Hendry Jones* (1956) returned to a more sympathetic view of the outlaw. Although the hero is called Jones and the scene is shifted to California, the novel is a retelling of the familiar Bonney saga. The Mexican theme is carried along by means of the girlfriend, Nika Machado. The law officers are villainous, and Neider too follows Burns in making the Olinger-character into a vindictive bully. That Neider was on firm ground, at least commercially speaking, was demonstrated when Marlon Brando bought the book and made a motion picture out of it.

Then in 1967, Amelia Bean published a historical novel entitled *Time for Outrage.* It is the story of the Lincoln County War, as seen through a character named Luke Bender rather than a biographical novel about Billy the Kid. In an "Author's Note," Mrs. Bean explains that the minor role assigned to Bonney is justified by the historical records: "Bonney never was at any time during the war a leader of any group or contingent." By deflating the Kid's role in this presumed struggle between good and evil, Mrs. Bean necessarily diminishes his Robin Hood reputation.

Biographers, on the other hand, continued to favor the sentimental interpretation established by Ferguson, Burns, and Otero. Frazier Hunt in *Tragic Days of Billy the Kid* (1956) described his hero as a romantic idealist. Hunt's reiteration of his major theme, which might be called A Motherless Boy in Search of Home, gives the book at times a soap-opera quality. "The slight figure of the homeless, motherless boy, cast in his desperate role, must have appealed to this romantic girl [Sallie Chisum] with the compassionate heart." The Kid remains a cheerful cherub through all his trials and tribulations, from the defeat of the McSween forces to the "betrayal" by Wallace and Garrett.

Hunt says that the Kid became an outlaw not because he was a saddle bum with an aversion for honest work, but because he had "a vision of himself as a valiant boy on horseback, fighting his lone battles seemingly against insurmountable odds." Partly, the "battle" is to carry on the ideals created for him by the father figure, John Tunstall. Like Burns, Hunt constructs a black-and-white picture of the Lincoln County War that makes the McSween gunmen crusaders for moral justice. "They had been on the right side, but unfortunately the right side was the side that had lost." The Kid's cattle thievery is thus explained by his continuing commitment to this laudable lost cause. While he is idealistic, others are mercenary. Pat Garrett in particular "wanted wealth, power, fame, recognition. And he had wanted it strongly enough to hire out his pistol to the highest bidder."

William Lee Hamlin also strengthened the Good Outlaw concept in his *True Story of Billy the Kid.* Published in 1959, this biography essentially accepts and repeats all the familiar conventions about the Kid's career. A lawyer by trade, Hamlin made an effort to incorporate legal and historical records in his "posthumous brief for Billy the Kid." But in attempting to make the book more readable, he fell into the trap of reconstructing scenes by using heavy doses of dialogue for which there is no documentation.

The method did give Hamlin ample opportunities to demonstrate that the Kid had been a good Samaritan. At the court of inquiry held to investigate Colonel Dudley's role in the Five Days Battle, Hamlin has the Kid saying that he stole Chisum cattle and sent the proceeds to the parents of McSween men killed in the fight.

> 'Very touching, if true,' [District Attorney] Rynerson said. 'No doubt you would have us believe you follow in the footsteps of Robin Hood of Sherwood Forest, stealing from the rich to give to the poor!' The boy was puzzled by the literary allusion. 'No sir,' he said earnestly, 'I never follow any man's lead. I don't know Mr. Hood or where he rides, but if he just rustled a few cows to help out a widowed mother, I hope the Sheriff's posse will never cut his trail.'

Movie makers, for their part, continued to supply the mass audience with varied interpretations of the outlaw's career. In 1949, Universal issued *The Kid from Texas.* The Kid in this version was war hero Audie Murphy, the star of numerous Hollywood shoot-'em-ups in the forties and fifties. Murphy made a good, if somewhat wooden, badman-hero, and the events of the Lincoln County War were restaged with fair accuracy. The one incongruous note was a romantic theme involving Mrs. McSween ("Cain" in the film), that made the Kid into a lovestruck mooncalf. But the basic characterization, derived from the Burns and Otero books, helped to reinforce the Robin Hood stereotype.

Then, within a few years of each other, two "Method" actors attempted experimental interpretations of the outlaw. In the 1958 film *Left-Handed Gun,* Paul Newman portrayed Bonney as a confused adolescent overly fond of pranks that sometimes resulted in death for others. The Kid's deep loyalty to "Tuntell" was the only theme drawn from history. In 1961, Marlon Brando essayed the role of "the Kid" in *One-Eyed Jacks,* a thinly disguised version of the Bonney saga based on Charles Neider's *Hendry Jones* novel. Brando was already too thick around the middle to make a convincing "Kid": in addition, he was more interested in the psychological dimensions of the outlaw's career than in a clear rendition of the legend. Neither of these "off-beat" films added much to the evolution of the Robin Hood concept. Both actors had such highly selective and personal views of the subject that history and tradition were pretty much ignored.

In 1961, the television industry took a stab at the outlaw theme with a series called *The Tall Man.* The title actually referred to Pat Garrett (Barry Sullivan) who was teamed with the Kid (Clu

Kris Kristofferson and James Coburn in a scene from *Pat Garrett and Billy the Kid* (1973). Courtesy Metro-Goldwyn-Mayer.

Gulager) in most of the thirty-minute episodes. The writer-producer of the series, Frank Price, firmly believed that the Kid was another Robin Hood rather than a Man-All-Bad. Consequently, Bonney was presented as a likeable, woman-chasing prankster. The scripts glossed over his many crimes, treating the relationship with Garrett more like a Tom-and-Jerry cartoon than a deadly struggle for survival.

In 1970, the Kid's heroic stature received ultimate sanctification: a John Wayne Western! The film was *Chisum,* with a rather paunchy Wayne playing the title role but with Billy the Kid [Geoffrey Deuel] a co-equal character. *Chisum* was an entertaining story, made up out of whole cloth. The Kid is given a Bible by Tunstall, and we find him quoting it on numerous occasions between bloodlettings. He also carves a wooden cross for Sallie Chisum, an episode in a contrived love affair between the two. Billy is shown shooting everybody in sight, including Morton and Baker, Sheriff

Brady, and even Jesse Evans. It is made clear, however, that all this gunwork is for a good cause, since Major Murphy and his cohorts are represented as the epitome of evil.

In 1973, the familiar saga was again recreated in MGM's *Pat Garrett and Billy the Kid,* with James Coburn as the relentless sheriff, and singing star Kris Kristofferson as the Kid. This version, which covers the period between the Kid's escape from Lincoln Jail and his shooting by Garrett, was based on the tradition that the two had been close friends at Fort Sumner. But Garrett becomes the tool of powerful banking and ranching interests in the Territory and so agrees to hunt down his former drinking companion. The unseen John Chisum is the true villain of the picture (compare with *Chisum* above), representing the "new order" that cannot tolerate the Kid's free-wheeling ways. The outlaw is certainly not idealized, being portrayed as a charming but lethal fellow to whom self-preservation was more important than either friendship or ethics. Many critics believe that this film is the closest Hollywood has come to an accurate rendering of the outlaw's character.

The cumulative effect of exposure in the various media was to make the Bonney legend familiar to most Americans. Probably all that the average citizen knew about New Mexico's history was that it had been the scene for Billy the Kid's escapades. In 1960, a university professor deplored the fact that although there were 437 published items on Billy the Kid, there was no satisfactory biography of any of New Mexico's eighteen territorial governors. One of these governors had been George Curry, who in his autobiography reiterated the theme by complaining that "tourists are all interested in the Kid rather than in the men who helped build a peaceful New Mexico." Alas! This imbalance is characteristic of all outlaw legendry. Jesse James is remembered, while the governors of Missouri are forgotten.

Bonney's fame as a "Robin Hood of the Southwest," may be undeserved, but his relationship with his mother, with Tunstall, and with the Mexican-Americans are all significant in under-standing why this legend eventually took hold. To be a hero, a man must revere his mother, and the Kid certainly meets the test with flying colors. Legendizers expanded upon the mother-theme, sometimes with excessive sentimentality. That fable of the Kid's stabbing the "filthy loafer" who had insulted her was also recited too many times. Even after discarding this tale, however, the biographer is still on safe ground if he maintains that the Kid was doing all right under her cheerful tutelage. Many have speculated that he might have followed the straight and narrow path had she lived for another year or so.

The Kid's relationship with John Tunstall, while also inflated by legend-builders, has some basis in fact. Bonney was a cool customer who looked out for himself first of all. At the same time, he was as loyal to his employer as the circumstances permitted. Probably the motive of revenge *after* Tunstall's murder was more important, in both history and legend, than loyalty *before* that event. Mrs. Ealy recorded in her diary that at Tunstall's funeral the Kid's "eyes almost frightened me; they appeared to glow with a deadly hatred. He later told me Mr. Tunstall had been the only friend he ever had except his mother." The fact that most people can understand this primitive emotion has helped to universalize the legend.

The Kid's friendship with the Mexican-Americans also has a basis in fact. It is of dubious validity only when it is cited to authenticate his reputation as a "folk" hero. Certainly the Kid had friends – and girlfriends – in the *casas.* But his hospitable reception is explained as much by age-old traditions and customs as by any belief that he was some kind of savior for the downtrodden. However, the fact that later generations believed he had been so idolized served to strengthen the Robin Hood concept.

The Kid's personality, both actual and reputed, is at the core of the legend. He had that redeeming sense of humor which distinguishes the Good Outlaw from the common thug. His apparent ability to crack a joke under even the most desperate circumstances gives him a touch of humanity that was lacking in the other hard-eyed renegades of the period. At the same time, he was cool in the face of extreme danger, an attribute Americans have liked to see in their sheriffs and detectives, as well as in their outlaws.

Nor can one ignore the Kid's diminutive physique. He "looked and acted a mere boy," said the Las Vegas *Gazette.* The nickname of "Kid" also added to the overall impression of boyishness. Contrast his measurements against the mansized frames of Pat Garrett or Lawrence G. Murphy, and the picture is the immemorial one of the "little guy" against the giants. He was hounded to his grave, so the legend has it, by powerful and physically stronger opponents who would not leave him be.

Finally, there is Bonney's ability to survive a succession of battles, ambushes, and imprisonments. One might call this his technical virtuosity. His friends are picked off one by one, but the Kid gallops on to further adventures, under "mystic protection" if we are to believe Walter Noble Burns. These escapes call forth a sneaking admiration most of us have for those who can outwit the authorities. If he had died early in the action, the Kid would have been forgotten.

The William Bonney of history was not a moronic killer, such as the dime novelists portrayed. He may have been psychopathic, but he was also a keen observer of events in Lincoln County. He had a sense of humor, was popular with women, and possessed other saving graces appropriate to a "Robin Hood."

THE DUBIOUS ROBIN HOOD:
BUTCH CASSIDY

Butch Cassidy is sometimes classed with the "Western Robin Hoods," but his is a borderline case. Neither the man nor his legend quite fit the pattern. To be sure, he was a highly successful bandit, and thus was a local celebrity of sorts in Utah and Wyoming. And he had the requisite personality: cheerful and outgoing rather than misanthropic or murderous. Yet he did not become the hero of a nationally known legend. Perhaps this was because his crimes could not be excused by any "social justice" idealism. Everyone knew he was a mere brigand, in the tradition of Captain Kidd or Morgan the Pirate.

Robert Leroy Parker was his original name. He was born on April 13, 1866, the first of many children in a ranching family, which lived in the remote Circle Valley of southern Utah. Just why he became an outlaw has not been satisfactorily explained. He was of Mormon upbringing, which ordinarily implies strict morality. But the well-known rebelliousness of his father, Maximillian Parker, may have been magnified in the son. Or he may have been influenced by Mike Cassidy (whose name he eventually "borrowed") a Parker ranch hand by day but an associate of outlaws by night. In any event, he grew into a stocky and sharp-witted youth who learned everything there was to know about riding, shooting, and branding.

By the time he was eighteen, Robert had left the family and become a prodigious pilferer of other people's livestock. Unlike the usual Robin Hood, he was not "driven" to crime by persecutors. Nor did he steal in order to protect poor homesteaders from greedy bankers or land monopolists, though such claims were later made in his behalf. He stole because he found it the easiest and most exciting way to get money.

Parker did try conventional jobs. At Telluride, Colorado, he was employed to pack ore by muleback down from the mines to the mill. But all the money around town was too much of a temptation. On June 24, 1889, he and two confederates grabbed over $10,000 in a lightning-fast noontime robbery of the local bank. The trio outsmarted the posse by riding across slick rock with the horses' feet wrapped in gunny sacks. They then hid out at Robbers' Roost, a tangled maze of canyons along the lower Green River in southeastern Utah. It was after this robbery that Parker adopted the name Cassidy, partly to protect his law-abiding kinfolk.

Parker-Cassidy lived in several Wyoming towns during the early 1890s. Brief employment as a butcher is said to account for his nickname, but his principal occupation was "horse trader." He enjoyed horse races, cracked jokes now and then, and was a hail-fellow-well-met at a number of bars and saloons in the region. As for women, he had several girlfriends, both married and unmarried. But this does not mean that Cassidy was incapable of violence. Like all outlaws, he was extremely dangerous when cornered.

On April 11, 1892, Marshal Bob Calverly of Evanston, Wyoming, arrested Cassidy on a horse theft charge. The marshal found his man lying on a bunk in a line cabin. "I told him I had a warrant for him and he said: 'Well, get to shooting,' and with that we both pulled our guns. I put the barrel of my revolver almost to his stomach, but it missed three times and, owing to the fact that there was another man between us, he failed to hit me. The fourth time I snapped the gun it went off and the bullet hit him in the upper part of the forehead and felled him." After Cassidy got out of prison he swore vengeance on Calverly. But he was never able to carry out his threat, because the marshal and his friends were just as determined and just as handy with guns as the outlaws.

After many postponements of his trial, Cassidy, on July 4, 1894, was convicted of horse stealing and sentenced to two years in the state penitentiary. However, he was pardoned on January 19, 1896, after promising Governor William A. Richards that he would keep hands off livestock and banks in the state. (But nothing was said about trains!) Cassidy was embittered at the time of his release, claiming, like so many others, that prison had "made" him an outlaw.

In the spring of 1896, the former convict was in Brown's Hole (or Brown's Park), forming a gang. This isolated region encompassed parts of three states: northeastern Utah, northwestern Colorado, and southern Wyoming. It was thus an ideal haven for outlaws, who could dodge back and forth across the boundaries. In addition, the residents of the area were so unsympathetic to lawmen that it was very dangerous for any of them to venture there.

Cassidy recruited the "Wild Bunch," known for their rowdiness and brazen thumb-to-nose defiance of the law. The twenty or so members included Elzy Lay, Harvey Logan, and Flat-Nose George Curry. A somewhat later addition was Harry Longabaugh, the so-called "Kid" from Sundance, Wyoming. Cassidy was undoubtedly the brains of the outfit and masterminded about a dozen bank and train holdups over the next five years. These commenced with the Montpelier (Idaho) bank on August 13, 1896, and ended with a Great Northern train near Wagner, Montana, on July 3, 1901. Usually the take was quite good, although the results were variable. The holdup of a Union Pacific train at Tipton, Wyoming, for example (August 29, 1900), netted only $50.40!

Cassidy's robberies were marked by intelligent planning and — generally — by smooth execution. He studied the layout of the bank or the timetable of the express train with great care and displayed coolness in managing the operation. After a train had been stopped, dynamite was used to blast open the express car doors. (Unlike Jesse James, Cassidy never bothered to rob passengers.) Then there would be a relay of fresh horses positioned beforehand along the escape route, so that posses were always outdistanced. The trail seemed to disappear in one of the hideouts along the "outlaw trail," which ran from Canada to Mexico. Brown's Hole, Robbers Roost, and Hole-in-the-Wall were three favorite haunts. The latter, located about thirty-five miles west of present-day Kaycee, Wyoming, is actually a broad north-to-south valley running alongside the Big Horn Mountains. Here congregated dozens of horse thieves, bank robbers, and other hard cases from throughout the West.

The outlaws of literature and legend steal from the rich and give to the poor. But, in Cassidy's case, it is difficult to find historical substantiation for such beneficence. This has been admitted even by those most sympathetic to the outlaw, such as his sister. On March 21, 1897, in another daring daylight holdup, Cassidy and Elzy Lay seized an $8,000 coal company payroll at Castle Gate, Utah. In her book, *Butch Cassidy, My Brother,* Lula Parker Betenson says that "the Castle Gate robbery had no Robin Hood motive; its proceeds would neither free a friend from prison nor avenge an injustice to a homesteader. It had been planned deliberately as a means of obtaining money for personal gain. Either my brother's conscience was hardening, or his hopes for freeing himself from the outlaw life were dimming. Maybe both of these things were happening."

As of 1900, Cassidy and the Sundance Kid had probably decided that their occupation was becoming so risky that they had better plan to pull out. The Union Pacific had formed the "Mounted Rangers," an elite posse that proved to be skillful and persistent. Also, the Pinkerton National Detective Agency had been hired by the express companies to track down the outlaws, and its operatives were getting closer to their quarry.

To create a nest egg for their exodus from the country, the two men recruited Bill Carver to help them hold up the First National Bank at Winnemucca, Nevada. On September 19th, they successfully carried out the job, escaping back to Brown's Hole with more than thirty-two thousand dollars. They then went to San Antonio, Texas, to spend some of the loot on new clothes and on the girls at Fanny Porter's Sporting House. With characteristic braggadocio, Cassidy had a photograph taken of some of the Wild Bunch during a visit to Fort Worth, a copy of which he mailed to the bank thanking them for their "contribution."

The holdup of the Great Northern train near Wagner, Montana, in July of 1901, is generally regarded as the last exploit of the Wild Bunch. Thereafter, the other members of the gang were tracked down by lawmen and either killed or imprisoned. But by February 1, 1902, Cassidy and the Sundance Kid were in New York City. Accompanying them was the Kid's girlfriend, Etta Place (if that really was her name). She was an attractive former schoolteacher, "and appears to be a refined type" says the Pinkerton report. "Jim Ryan" and "Mr. and Mrs. Harry Place" were the names the three used in the city. They visited Tiffany's, had their pictures taken, and then took a boat to Argentina, a country which, at that time, had no extradition treaty with the United States.

From this point on, the trail becomes obscure. The traditional story is that Cassidy and Longabaugh ran a ranch in Argentina for several years and then moved their operations to Bolivia. But there they reverted to the old pattern and began robbing mine payrolls and banks. By this time Etta Place had disappeared as mysteriously as she had come. The two men were supposedly killed in a gun battle with soldiers at San Vicente, Bolivia, early in 1909. There would be persistent stories that Cassidy had not been killed, but the Pinkerton Agency, which had had operatives working on the case, was satisfied that the two outlaws had been slain.

For the next sixty years, from 1909 to 1969, there was little in-

Some of the Wild Bunch at Fort Worth in 1900. Left to right Harry "Sundance Kid" Longabaugh, Bill Carver, Ben Kilpatrick, Harvey Logan, and Butch Cassidy. Courtesy Western History Collections, University of Oklahoma Library.

terest in Butch Cassidy. There was no cluster of novels, biographies, or movies comparable to those about Jesse James or Billy the Kid. In his home territory there were some oral traditions of the Robin Hood type. The well-worn anecdote of the Outlaw and the Poor Widow, for example, had become well established as part of Cassidy folklore by about 1930. And, after the New Deal years, some people even convinced themselves as one woman put it, that Butch "took care of more poor people than FDR." But the outlaw was not well known outside the mountain West. In 1930, an article by Arthur Chapman did appear in *Elks Magazine,* and it included a melodramatic description of the Bolivian shoot-out. This sparked a flurry of other stories, but as these all appeared in publications of the *National Police Gazette* type, they did not affect Cassidy historiography in a major way.

It wasn't until 1938 that the first serious historical effort was published. This was Charles Kelly's *The Outlaw Trail: A History of Butch Cassidy and His Wild Bunch*. Kelly was a conscientious researcher, and he gathered a substantial amount of information on a man whom he regarded as a Rocky Mountain Robin Hood: "While he never consciously robbed the rich to feed the poor, he did perform many acts of generosity. So far as we know, he never killed a man during his entire career, until his last stand. That in itself makes him outstanding among outlaws." But the book did not result in the elevation of Cassidy to national stature. That's because it was not published in New York or Chicago, but in Salt Lake City, and in a privately printed edition of only one thousand copies. Its only effect was to cause an uproar in Utah, because Kelly had named practically every man who had ridden the "outlaw trail," and many of them were still alive and hopping mad about his comments.

The outlaw's historical "non-importance" remained unchanged until 1969. In that year, Twentieth Century Fox released the film *Butch Cassidy and the Sundance Kid*, with Paul Newman and Robert Redford in the lead roles. This has been the most financially successful Western ever made. By 1978 it had grossed 75 million dollars. So popular was it that the studio wanted to make the usual sequel, but this was impossible because the two characters had been killed in the final reel. However, in 1978 a "prequel" was made. Entitled *Butch and Sundance: the Early Days*, it featured two younger actors (Tom Berenger and William Katt) and was set in the 1890s.

Newman and Redford portrayed the two outlaws as wise-cracking clowns. They make fun of each other, of Bolivia, of conventional society. In fact, the film was written more as a comedy than as an outlaw story. Nevertheless, scriptwriter William Goldman claimed historical authenticity for his screenplay: "Not that it matters, but most of what follows is true." Actually, very little of it was true to fact. The depiction of Cassidy as a basically harmless and genial individual conflicts with the record, as revealed for example in his attempt at revenge on Bob Calverly. He was also misportrayed as being so generous that he was adored by everybody except sheriffs and railroaders. As Edward Lipton said in his review for *Film Daily*, "the projection of humanity and warmth tends to obfuscate the fact that these are after all immoral men."

The film planted the idea that desperate outlaws go around singing lighthearted tunes, in this case *Raindrops Keep Falling on My Head.* Goldman's script says "this song will not be loud. But it will be poignant. And pretty as hell." This in a story about hardened criminals! Of course, Butch Cassidy didn't actually sing the song; it was only background music in a scene where he and Etta Place cavort on a bicycle. But a whole generation of film goers associates the name of Butch Cassidy with this "pretty" song, which has become a popular-music classic.

The success of the movie in turn prompted revised versions of Cassidy's historical importance. The actual man was so gifted that if he'd only gotten the breaks he might have become a successful businessman, a congressman, or even a senator from the state of Utah! But such evaluations were not based on any startling discoveries of hidden manuscripts, or revelations that Butch Cassidy was really a son of Brigham Young. Indeed, much of the material about him had been available for years, but there was little interest in it. But some of the millions of people who saw the motion picture were hungry for information about the actual outlaw. So, suddenly, thanks to Hollywood, there was a market that had not been there before.

Publishers, led by the university presses, responded to the demand. By 1975 the Brigham Young University Press had issued Mrs. Betenson's *Butch Cassidy, My Brother,* a combination memoir and biography by the outlaw's then-ninety-one-year-old sister. Her manuscript had apparently been awaiting a publisher for at least five years. But it required some polishing by a professional writer (Dora Flack) and the impact of the film to effect its publication. In fact, a preface by Robert Redford and illustrations from the movie set showed the close relationship of Hollywood and history in this instance. Similarly, the University of Oklahoma Press's publication of Larry Pointer's *In Search of Butch Cassidy* in 1977 and the issuance of Robert Redford's own *The Outlaw Trail* in 1978 are both attributable to the movie's influence.

Much of the material about Cassidy is folkloric rather than historical. He was the subject of oral traditions comparable to those about Jesse James. Besides the classic Poor Widow tales, there are those in which the outlaw displays bravado by entering towns,

Robert Redford and Paul Newman as they appeared in *Butch Cassidy and the Sundance Kid*. Courtesy 20th Century-Fix.

despite the presence of law officers. Following the Castle Gate robbery, a posse stumbled across an outlaw camp and killed a man they mistakenly believed was Butch Cassidy. The body was brought to Price, Utah, for burial. When Cassidy heard about it, he decided to attend the event. Friends brought him to town in the bed of a wagon that was covered with tarpaulin and that had peepholes cut in the sides. Butch was quite touched by seeing some women shed a few tears at the "funeral." History or folklore? It's hard to tell, but Robin Hood went to Nottingham and thumbed his nose at the sheriff, too.

"Resurrection" tales are another way in which folklore pays tribute to the badman, since they confer indestructibility on him. Stories that Cassidy had not been killed in South America were in oral circulation for years, despite the published reports of his demise. Such stories formed the core of both the Pointer and Betenson books. Pointer investigated the possibility that William T. Phillips of Spokane, Washington, had been Cassidy. In 1934, Phillips wrote a manuscript entitled "The Bandit Invincible, the Story of Butch Cassidy." At that time an unsuccessful effort had been made to publish the manuscript as a book and/or sell it to one of the motion picture studios. It contained so many "inside" details of the outlaw's career that a number of people believed Phillips to have been Cassidy. Pointer himself became one of those believers after analyzing all the pro and con evidence.

Lula Parker Betenson decided to break a forty-year silence and tell the truth about her brother. He had indeed come back to Circle Valley in 1925 for a visit with the family. He had then moved on and "had died in the Northwest in the fall of 1937." However, she went on, "he was not the man who was known as William Phillips, reported to be Butch Cassidy." She refused to divulge what name he *had* used, or where he had been buried.

Ordinarily, one would discount such stories, since they are so much a part of the classic folklore pattern. Jesse James, Billy the Kid, and John Dillinger had not really died; the corpses were those of look-alikes. But, after all, Mrs. Betenson was the outlaw's sister. Pointer's Mr. Phillips is a much more dubious candidate. Aside from various factual inaccuracies, about half of the Phillips manuscript describes Cassidy's acts of charity, including two Poor Widow episodes. The abundance of these anecdotes suggests that the document has folkloric rather than historical importance. In any case, speculation about the outlaw's possible return-from-the-dead helped to keep his legend alive.

In the Butch Cassidy literature, the hero worshippers have outnumbered the debunkers. In fact, unlike other outlaws, there have been no debunkers. This is explainable in part because the actual man did have unusual qualities for someone in his trade. He defied and laughed at the agents of big business – the banks and the railroads – that were seen by many as the symbols of a corporate take-over of the West. He not only took from the takers, but he lived to a comfortable old age if one believes the "resurrection" stories. Then, too, folklore enlarged his virtues to some extent, seeing him as a do-gooder. But Hollywood is primarily responsible for transforming the tough ex-convict into an appealing rogue and giving him the nationwide audience that is necessary for lasting renown. It is a bit early to conclude that Butch Cassidy will become another American Robin Hood. But the prospects look pretty good.

END OF TRAIL: PRETTY BOY FLOYD

The Great Depression of the 1930s briefly recreated the classic social conditions from which Robin Hood legends emerge. But it recreated them for the last time. Improved communications, more efficient police forces, and increasing urbanization were some of the developments that would bring an end to rural banditry. Then, too, the organized gangs that were forming in the cities during the same decade represented a methodical, businesslike approach to crime that allowed no room for individual enterprise. Hence the "Public Enemies" of the Thirties were in a sense the last of the line.

The decade's likeliest candidate for Robin Hood status is the Oklahoma bank robber, "Pretty Boy" Floyd. His long record in crime and the popular reaction to those crimes fit the age-old pattern most closely.

Charley Arthur Floyd was born on a farm in Bartow County, Georgia, on February 3, 1904. The large family migrated to Oklahoma within a year, and the youth was raised near the little towns of Akins and Sallisaw. These were in the heart of the Cookson Hills, a primitive area of deep gullies, wild prairie stretches, and oak-studded foothills that merge into the Ozarks. Because of their isolation, the Hills had been a natural rendezvous for outlaws since the 1870s. Floyd grew up listening to stories of how Jesse James, Bill Doolin, and the Dalton brothers had outwitted the law and escaped to hideouts in the locality. The clannish people there had an inborn dislike for the officers, an attitude explained in part by the fact that many of the families had been "moonshiners" for several generations. Thus a bank robber could expect to find refuge with this largely sympathetic population.

The Floyds were honest hill folk, the mother being a diligent worker for the Baptist Church. But the father, Walter Floyd, was illiterate, and youths in the area had little opportunity for economic or educational advancement. Charley got as far as the sixth grade in school, but he was more adept at squirrel shooting than at reading and figuring. The young dropout kept "working in the sand-hills for a cornbread living," as his sister Mary put it. He grew into a chunky, beetle-browed roustabout, who nevertheless always kept his black hair carefully combed. He became known as a "heller," who enjoyed the powerful, though illegally brewed, "Choctaw beer." He also got along very well with young women, who seemed to find him attractive. At nineteen, Charley married a farmer's daughter from the town of Bixby, sixteen-year-old Ruby Hargraves. A son, Jack Dempsey Floyd, was born, but the couple were divorced in 1925. Floyd was unwilling or unable to support his family by farming in the red claybank around Sallisaw. So, in 1925, he "followed the harvest" north, a common practice for migrant laborers in those years. But, instead of staying in the fields, he held up a bakery company payroll in St. Louis and netted $12,500 to launch his career in crime.

Floyd returned home and began spending money. An alert marshal hauled him in for questioning, and he was shortly tried and found guilty of the payroll robbery. As he later admitted to a newspaper reporter, "I was a green country kid that got caught on a job." He was sentenced to five years in the Missouri state penitentiary. The records show that he entered prison on September 16, 1925, and was released on December 8, 1926, thus having served about one year and three months.

The Floyd family version was that after Charley came back from prison he was "persecuted" – an immemorial justification for outlawry. According to his wife, Ruby, he lost his job with an oil company in the Seminole fields after being arrested on suspicion of a store holdup. His mother, Mrs. Maymie Floyd, believed that her boy was driven to further crime by constant harassment: "Charles has not done one-thousandth of the crimes he has been accused of." Floyd himself had the same idea. In one letter to the editor of the Kansas City *Star* he said, "I'm not as bad as they say I am: they just wouldn't let me alone after I got out."

The young ex-con gravitated to Kansas City, Missouri, a wide-open town during the heyday of the Tom Pendergast machine. The police there began to take notice of Floyd, beginning on May 6, 1927, when they arrested him for vagrancy. Just how he made his living over the next two years is uncertain. Underworld gossip was that he was a "front man" for the Syndicate, which ran gambling and prostitution rings in the city. It was also believed that he was a driver for the bootlegging operations in the region.

By the beginning of 1930, Floyd had graduated to bank robbery, the apex in the pyramid of crime. He and two partners hit a series of small banks in northern Ohio. But on March 11th their car crack-

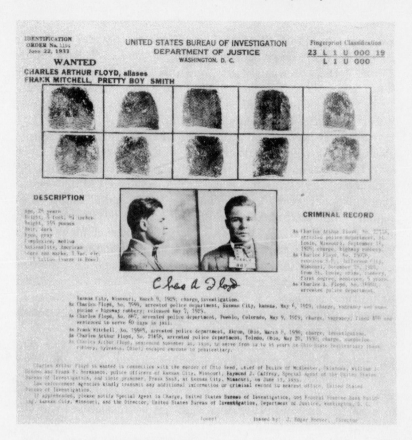

Prison photo of Pretty Boy Floyd. The bow tie indicates part of the reason for the "Pretty Boy" nickname. Courtesy Wide World Photos.

ed up while trying to elude police pursuit, and Floyd was captured. He was convicted of robbing the bank at Sylvania, Ohio, and was sentenced to fifteen years in the state penitentiary. On the train taking him to Columbus, Floyd suddenly jumped through an open window, rolled down the embankment, and sprinted away into the darkness before the guards knew what had happened. Shades of Billy the Kid!

Floyd managed to get back to Kansas City, where he holed up in one of the numerous gangland hideouts. It was the madam of this establishment, a Mrs. Sadie Ash, who conferred the immortal nickname of "Pretty Boy" on him. Floyd did not like the name, which he once described as "all a joke anyway." Back in the Cookson Hills he was always known as "Charley" or "Chock," the latter being a reference to his taste for Choctaw beer. But newspaper reporters liked the moniker, and they henceforth used it in their stories on the elusive gunman. And it did reflect Floyd's concern over the impression he made on women, in particular on Beulah Baird, who was also rooming at the Ash place.

By the spring of 1931, Floyd was back in Ohio robbing banks, this time in partnership with William ("Bill-the-Killer") Miller. Beulah Baird also went along as cook, bottle washer, and all-around companion. The men pulled several robberies, but then on April 15th things went haywire. Two officers spotted them coming out of a store on the main street of Bowling Green, Ohio. In the exchange of gunfire, Floyd killed Patrolman Ralph Kastner, but the other officer riddled Miller. Floyd managed to get away, leaving the woman behind in his haste, but it was a close call. The bloody shoot-out brought "Pretty Boy" to the attention of the nation's newspaper readers and raised his status to that of "Public Enemy."

Once again Floyd had to seek cover in Kansas City. On the evening of July 21st, he found that even there he was far from secure. Federal prohibition agents following a tip raided a bootlegger's hideout. Much to their surprise, they encountered "Pretty Boy," and as usual he came out firing revolvers. Agent Curtis Burke was killed, and another man was severly wounded. This time, with the "heat" really on, the fugitive headed for home territory: the Cookson Hills.

Floyd emerged from his lair in the fall of 1931 and committed a series of bank robberies that kept law officers in a dither. Part of his success may be credited to utilization of modern technology, particularly the Ford V-8 and the submachine gun. Where Jesse James had secured the finest horses available (usually by stealing them), Floyd had similarly gotten hold of the fastest and most dependable automobiles around. He was also known to have worn a bulletproof vest and a steel skullcap at times. It seems that outlaws not only keep up with technology, they are often a step ahead of the police in this regard.

Floyd never had a gang, although newspapermen often used the word. Familiar as he was with the fate of Jesse James, he may have felt that the larger the group the greater the chance it would include a turncoat or informer. So he worked with only one partner. In 1931-32 this was George Birdwell, a one-time evangelist preacher who had become so addicted to John Barleycorn that he had turned to crime to support the habit. The usual method of operation was for the two men to enter a bank in very nonchalant fashion, never wearing disguises. Floyd would then cover everybody with the sub-machine gun which he kept cradled in his arms, while Birdwell went behind the teller's cage and collected the cash. Often they took bank employees as hostages, who were left off a few miles down the road.

It was a system that worked very well in one country town after another. The take was never very large at any one bank. For example, on January 14, 1932, they held up banks at Paden, Oklahoma, and at Castle, Oklahoma, taking $2,500 from the first and $2,000 at the second. Yet, at the time of Floyd's death, the newspapers estimated that he had netted a total of $50,000 in Oklahoma alone, and dollars were worth a lot more in the Depression years. At any rate, the Oklahoma Bankers Association became concerned enough to offer a reward of $5,000 for the capture of "Pretty Boy."

The state government also took the home-grown outlaw quite seriously. Lieutenant Governor Robert Burns, in posting a $1,000 state reward offer, said that "this is a desperate case. This man has terrorized the entire eastern-central section of Oklahoma with his outlawry. Already six killings and ten bank robberies have been charged to him. He must be stopped." With characteristic effrontery, Floyd sent Burns a postcard which read: "You either withdraw that one thousand at once or suffer the consequences. No kidding. I have robbed no one but moneyed men. Floyd."

The police tried their hardest to nail the desperado. Erv Kelley was a veteran law officer who in 1932 was a state special agent. He was determined to collect the reward money, but in trying to take Floyd he bit off more than he could chew. With other officers he set up an ambush at the home of the outlaw's father-in-law near Bixby. When Floyd and Birdwell drove up to the house in the early morning hours of April 9th, Kelley stepped out and ordered them to surrender. He was answered by a fatal blast of submachine-gun fire, and the outlaws escaped despite the usual "hail of bullets" fired at their car by the other officers. Kelley left five children, and the State Police Officers' Association sent his widow a check for $50.

The shooting cost Floyd scores of friends, since Kelley was a

popular man in eastern Oklahoma. Still he had enough of a following to be sure of a welcome reception anywhere east of the
Seminole oilfields. The loyalty of the hill people to their own kind,
and the corresponding suspicion of "outsiders," worked to the
outlaw's advantage. The Hillbilly, said one newspaper reporter, "is
as uncommunicative as a deaf and dumb Indian when somebody is
seeking information." Then, too, Floyd spent the money from his
robberies among the destitute farmers of the sand hills, and they
protected him in return.

Much of Floyd's renown was derived from the fact that his career
peaked during the depth of the Great Depression. The farmers of
Oklahoma could not meet the payments on their mortgages when
hard times came. The banks thus foreclosed many farms. Large
absentee companies took possession and brought in machinery for
large-scale agriculture. Some of those forced off the land piled into
their jalopies and joined the famous "Okie" emigration to California.
Those who remained blamed their troubles on the "system," which
they considered to be run by hardhearted capitalists who cared
nothing for the little fellow. They made a hero out of Floyd because
he personified their idea of social justice.

There is plenty of evidence, recorded in the newspapers of the
day, that the outlaw did "give to the poor." W.R. Draper filed a story
for the United Press from Tahlequah, in which he reported that
"Floyd is all the farm relief they need down here in the Cookson
Hills, it would seem. When he has money, the hill folk say, every
needy person gets a slice. The Floyd generosity appears to be more
than legendary, because every merchant in the backwoods who has
been interviewed by this correspondent affirms the story." Vivian
Brown, a reporter for the *Oklahoma News* and a native of the
Cookson Hills, was also satisfied that "there is much to support the
picture of Floyd as a modern Robin Hood. Like the famed
marauder of the English forests, he took money from those who
had it – the banks – and divided the proceeds among the poor.
The penniless tenant farmers kept their mouths shut; they had no
scruples about taking contraband wrested from bankers."

So the hill people's loyalty to "Pretty Boy" kept him alive. He was
lucky, cunning, and ruthless; all attributes of the successful outlaw.
But, without their support, he would never have lasted as long as
he did. Their loyalty is clearly revealed by the fact that they never
turned him in, despite the $6,000 in reward money offered by the

bankers and the state. The absence of any "betrayal" is a remarkable variation from the usual Robin Hood pattern, and this makes Floyd a rather unique outlaw.

So Floyd continued to enjoy unparalleled success. During the summer and fall of 1932, he and Birdwell robbed an estimated fifty banks in Oklahoma and adjacent states. (The exact number is difficult to determine, since some of the robberies attributed to him were undoubtedly committed by others.) The police set up roadblocks, but Floyd would cut fences and drive through the cornfields to regain the safety of the hills. On two occasions, the officers got close enough to fire into his car, but the desperados' bulletproof vest – so they said – saved him. A legend of invincibility began to take shape. The hillbilly radio programs started playing a new tune, "Pretty Boy Floyd, the Phantom Terror," which expanded his will-o'-the-wisp reputation. Newspapers also called him "the hoodoo hoodlum."

Most galling of all to the police was Floyd's impudence and braggadocio. Newsboys were only half joking when they shouted, "Four officers escape from Pretty Boy!" Farmers chuckled when the outlaw was quoted as saying, "there's a chief of police at Seminole who stays up twenty-four hours a day trying to figure out where I am so he can be somewhere else." On August 4, 1932, Floyd picked up a former Tulsa policeman named H.W. Nave on the highway, stripped him of his clothing, and drove away laughing. Furthermore, he appeared openly at country dances, at funerals, and even (say some accounts) at Baptist church services; all to the chagrin of frustrated detectives.

Even though his wife had divorced him, Floyd continued to see her and his son. The three of them lived together in Tulsa for a time during 1932. Floyd claimed that they lived across the street from federal agents, who were unable to recognize him. One evening, when Floyd took his son to the movies, the cashier stopped him in a long line of customers. The outlaw started to reach for his automatic, but the cashier simply asked him if he thought the child wasn't too young to see the picture. *Dracula* was playing.

So confident did the outlaw become that he decided to visit his hometown. On November 1st, he and Birdwell rolled into Sallisaw, greeted old friends and acquaintances on the street – and then robbed the bank! They got only $2,500, but, as one newspaperman said, "it was like the hometown performance of a great actor who has made good on Broadway."

The successful partnership was terminated when Birdwell decided to rob the bank at the Negro community of Boley, located between the earlier target towns of Paden and Castle. Floyd warned his sidekick that the place was too well guarded. But on November 22nd, the ex-preacher and two other men tried to pull it off. They were gunned down by citizens who, it turned out, all had rifles and shotguns for the opening of the hunting season that very day!

In 1933, Floyd's working life became much riskier because of the increased activity of the Federal Bureau of Investigation. State police had been hampered in their pursuit of criminals because they could not cross state lines. The FBI, however, was a national organization empowered to follow bank robbers wherever the trail led. Headed since 1924 by J. Edgar Hoover, the FBI in the early thirties was still a small and often amateurish organization. Yet the outlaw soon found that "the Feds" were more formidable antagonists than the small town sheriffs.

Sometime in the spring of 1933, the outlaw picked up a new lieutenant. This was Adam Richetti, a cold-eyed former oilfield worker. On June 16th, the two men appeared in Bolivar, Missouri, to have their car repaired. Polk County Sheriff Jack Killingsworth happened to stroll into the garage, and was immediately covered by Floyd and made into a hostage. He accompanied the two fugitives on a roundabout auto trip before being released in the Kansas City area. Floyd drank "moonshine" liquor from a jar, and treated Killingsworth to a soliloquy about the life of crime. He expressed deep hatred for the cops, who had never "left him alone," but admitted that sooner or later they would kill him.

Floyd's known presence in Kansas City accounts for the theory that he was a participant in the infamous Union Station Massacre of June 17th. Frank Nash was a veteran bank robber and prison escapee who was being taken back to Leavenworth penitentiary by Federal agents. As the party was getting into cars at the station, three men with submachine guns ordered them to "Get 'em up," but then immediately opened fire. Three police officers and an FBI agent were killed, and two other agents were wounded. Frank Nash also died in the fusillade.

The FBI, understandably enraged by the attack on its own people, jumped to the conclusion that Floyd and Richetti were involved. But they never proved their case, and it now appears that

Floyd was not guilty of this particular crime. The actual gunmen were killed by the syndicate for having bungled their assignment; or else for knowing too much. One of these men, William "Solly" Weissman, bore a marked resemblance to Floyd. It is no surprise that a distraught and harried Travelers Aid Society worker, Mrs. Lottie West, identified a photo of Floyd as the "heavy set man" she had seen loitering in the station before the shootings. This was all that the FBI needed to charge the notorious Pretty Boy with being the lead killer.

However, the job was too much as variance with the usual Floyd pattern. He was always loud-mouthed about his exploits, but on two occasions he specifically denied having been in on the massacre. On the 21st, Captain Thomas J. Higgins of the Kansas City Police received a postcard in the mail which said, "I – Charles Floyd – want it made known that I did not participate in the massacre of officers at Kansas City." Again, when Floyd was shot by FBI men in Ohio the next year, almost his last words when queried about the episode were, "I didn't do it. I wasn't in on it." In this instance, it seems that Ruby Floyd was right when she maintained that the government "hung the Union Station massacre on him."

The last months of the outlaw's career were marked by gun battles and escapes in Oklahoma, Iowa, and Ohio. On October 11, 1934, two police officers spotted Floyd and Richetti at a farmhouse near Cresco, Iowa. The fugitives escaped after exchanging fire with the officers. Then, on the 20th, police at Wellsville in eastern Ohio, got a tip that two suspicious characters were loitering outside town. When the chief of police saw the two men, he immediately recognized one of them as Floyd who, with his usual catlike reflexes, pulled an automatic and started firing. Surprisingly, one of the men, Richetti, was captured. Floyd plunged into nearby woods, having pulled off another of his seemingly endless series of escapes. This time, however, the end was near, and he remained at large for only two days.

FBI agents under Melvin Purvis, head of the Chicago office, joined the intensive manhunt. On the 22nd, the lawmen heard that Floyd had been seen at a farmhouse near East Liverpool. Two carloads of officers surrounded the farm, and as they closed in Floyd attempted to escape across a cornfield. He was riddled with submachine gun bullets. The outlaw lived for about fifteen minutes, and under questioning by Purvis admitted his identity, but denied complicity in the Kansas City Massacre.* The FBI never accepted the disclaimer, and Adam Richetti was subsequently executed for his presumed role in the affair. At any rate, one of the most predatory and elusive of the Depression-era gunmen was finally put out of business. And in the Wild West tradition to which he really belonged, he died with his shoes on.

The story of Pretty Boy's death was important enough to make the front page of the New York *Times,* which described him as having been "the most dangerous man alive." In the wire service accounts, J. Edgar Hoover was quoted as saying that Floyd was "just a yellow rat who needed extermination." Many people shared this view, but Floyd's friends back in Oklahoma saw it differently. W.R. Draper filed a story for the United Press which said that

> . . .as news filtered into the country, friends from the backwoods came and went in their rickety old motor cars. Many of them left the Floyd cottage. . .with bowed heads, the women brushing away tears. Charley had been a meal ticket to many of these folks during the depression years. To others, he was just a country boy who had taken the wrong road.

In these contrasting opinions, one sees the familiar signposts of a Robin Hood legend.

Floyd was buried at Sallisaw on October 18th. "He shore looks natural-like," commented one of the family upon viewing the corpse. For the funeral service, the Baptist preacher, W.E. Rockett, took as his text the last words of Christ on the cross, "It is finished." The rites were hardly private, as an estimated twenty thousand people jammed the roads for miles around, trying to get to the cemetery. Teenaged boys and girls wept over the coffin of their fallen hero. The crowd trampled on the other graves, picked leaves off the trees as far as they could reach, and collected small rocks for souvenirs. One woman who was there recalled having lost all the buttons from her dress during the pushing and squirming. The Floyd family sat through it all with the stolid, undemonstrative attitude of the hill people.

The Robin Hood folk tradition, already well formed during the outlaw's life, continued to flourish after his death. People in eastern Oklahoma named their children after him. They told of how he had kept a rural school open by supplying it with firewood, of how he had left large bills under the plate after dining with backwoods

---

*Years later, one of the local policemen charged that the FBI agents "executed" Floyd because he refused to answer questions.

families. Women especially remembered "Charley" as a prince of a fellow. One told of how he had commandeered her car to pull off a robbery, and then courteously returned it at the end of the day. Another recalled that he had stopped a car in which his mother was riding, but when told that the car's occupants were poor and had no money, had apologized and let them go on their way.

One Oklahoman who popularized the "good badman" idea was the great folk singer and composer, Woody Guthrie. Born and raised in Okemah, not far from the Cookson Hills, Guthrie's life had been filled with enough hardship and bad luck so that he could sympathize with an outcast like Floyd. (His mother had died in a mental hospital, and the father had suffered disastrous financial reverses.) So his ballad of "Pretty Boy Floyd" incorporates many of the timeless themes found in earlier songs about Robin Hood and Jesse James: the outlaw driven to crime by some provocation, his idealized character, his role as an agent of social justice. Sung to a tune approximating that of "Raggle Taggle Gypsies," the text is:

> If you'll gather 'round me, children,
> A story I will tell
> Of Pretty Boy Floyd, an outlaw
> Oklahoma knew him well.
>
> It was in the town of Shawnee,
> It was Saturday afternoon;
> His wife beside him in his wagon
> As into town they rode.
>
> There a deputy sheriff approached him
> In a matter rather rude
> Using vulgar words of language
> And his wife she overheard.
>
> Pretty Boy grabbed a log chain,
> And the deputy grabbed a gun;
> And in the fight that followed,
> He laid that deputy down.
>
> He took to the trees and timber
> On that Canadian River's shore;
> And Pretty Boy found a welcome
> At a many a farmer's door.
>
> There's many a starving farmer
> The same old story told,
> How this outlaw paid their mortgage
> And saved their little home.

Others tell you 'bout a stranger
That came to beg a meal,
And underneath his napkin
Left a thousand dollar bill.

It was in Oklahoma City,
It was on a Christmas Day,
There came a whole car load of groceries
With a letter that did say:

"You say that I'm an outlaw,
You say that I'm a thief;
Here's a Christmas dinner
For the families on relief."

Now as through this world I ramble,
I see lots of funny men;
Some will rob you with a six-gun
And some with a fountain pen.

But as through your life you travel,
As through your life you roam,
You won't never see an outlaw
Drive a family from their home.*

This ballad is a valuable document in the social history of the Depression years. Yet, it did not flourish in the oral tradition of the down-and-outers. Rather, it was a most popular ballad with middle class liberals. Singers such as Pete Seeger and Joan Baez presented it in concerts and included it in their recordings. Miss Baez sang it in a lyrical style that had enormous appeal to her young contemporaries in the 1960s. They were responding to mythology-in-the-making.

Not all Oklahomans shared Guthrie's adulation for the outlaw. In 1934, some folks in Adair County were singing another "Pretty Boy Floyd":

Pretty Boy was born in the Oklahoma hills
Where the beautiful flowers grow wild.
He was christened "Charles Arthur" by his parents so proud,
To thank God for their beautiful child.

By the side of his cradle his mother would sing,
Never dreaming of sorrow he'd bring.
But a mother's heart is broken when a boy grows to a man;
It's been there true since time first began.

---

*PRETTY BOY FLOYD
  by Woody Guthrie
  ©Copyright 1961, by Fall River Music, Inc.
  All Rights Reserved. Used by Permission.

Pretty Boy was twenty when he married his young wife;
She was only sixteen summers old,
He then went to work in a bakery shop out there
Where he drifted away from the fold.

Left his young wife in Bixby in Nineteen Twenty-Four,
Went to Kansas to try to earn more.
Then he went to St. Louis, got in bad company,
And wound up in the penitentiary.

Well, he served his time, then he went to Ohio
Killed a man and was sentenced again
But he didn't serve his time that the jury sentenced him,
For he jumped from a fast-moving train.

Kansas City was his next, and he took it on the run;
Killed two brothers with his careless gun.
Then he killed Mr. Burke, and man named Mr. Wilson,
And he left Kansas City on the run.

Ohio again, where he killed Mr. Cashman,
Spreading fear all along his crooked path,
Then he went back home, got into another row,
Killed the sheriff who had stirred up his row.

'Twas the last trip to Ohio, oh! for this wicked fool;
He was shot dead eight miles from Liverpool,
Pretty Boy will learn on that last great day
That a life filled with crime doesn't pay.

Most people outside Oklahoma, however, knew Floyd through
Guthrie's ballad or the best-selling novel by John Steinbeck, *Grapes
of Wrath* (1939). Steinbeck had heard the story of Pretty Boy from
the "Okie" emigres in California during the late thirties. He adopted
their sympathetic view of the outlaw in toto. The character, Ma
Joad, voices the familiar idea that he was "driven" to crime by in-
tolerable provocations. "He done a little bad thing an' they hurt 'im,
caught 'im an' hurt 'im so he was mad, an' the next bad thing he
done was mad, an' they hurt 'im again." When such powerful artists
as Guthrie and Steinbeck helped to romanticize the outlaw, J. Edgar
Hoover's less imaginative "yellow rat" concept lost ground.

Inevitably, movie producers capitalized on the appeal of the
legend. Hoover must have been shocked indeed when the film,
Pretty Boy Floyd, was released in 1960. The synposis described
Floyd as a "sagebush Robin Hood," and in the story he makes a
point of robbing only moneyed men. His partner, Richetti, asks
him at one point, "Are you some kind of a Robin Hood?" Floyd

replies that he does not want to rob bank clerks who have "holes in their shoes." Much was made of the "Pretty Boy" appellation, and Floyd, portrayed by a handsome actor, John Ericson, is incessantly combing his hair. The script did follow the major outlines of Floyd's career with reasonable fidelity. It also managed to capture some of the flavor of the Depression years.

Then, in 1970, American International Pictures issued *A Bullet for Pretty Boy*. It starred Fabian Forte, a former teen-age idol who was badly miscast in the role. He was too innocent and virginal-looking to make a convincing desperado. The script changes the bragging cop-killer of history into a sensitive youth who committed crimes with great reluctance. There were some recognizable historical episodes, but a prefatory statement that "this is the true story of Pretty Boy Floyd, 1904-1934," was unsubstantiated.

The most successful cinematic recreation of the outlaw's career came in 1974. This was the American Broadcasting Company's made-for-television movie entitled *The Story of Pretty Boy Floyd*. Martin Sheen acted the lead in what was essentially a character study rather than a shoot-'em-up. Floyd becomes an outlaw because he is unwilling to accept the ruthless exploitation of his labor in the oilfields. During his career in crime, he remains a dutiful son and husband, and is regarded as a hero in his home territory. The film was so carefully researched – being based on interviews with Floyd's surviving relatives – that it represented an interesting blend of documentary and drama.

The movie seems to have triggered a controversy about the FBI's role in the outlaw's demise. The Associated Press published an interview with Chester C. Smith, a retired policeman of East Liverpool, Ohio, who claimed that Floyd was deliberately shot to death because he wouldn't talk. The Bureau in 1974 was under something of a cloud because of its apparent complicity in the Watergate scandal. So it is not surprising that newspaper editorials, such as the *Los Angeles Times* article of October 28th on "Questions for the FBI," asked that the Bureau refute the charge. Director Clarence Kelley promptly did so in an official statement. Yet Smith stuck to his story. Five years later, in another interview, he repeated his claim that Melvin Purvis had ordered agents to finish off the wounded outlaw. Whatever the truth, the dispute helped to keep Floyd's name before the public.

Floyd's credentials as a Robin Hood candidate are much better than those of any of his outlaw contemporaries. Historical records and folk traditions are abundant enough, and they are close together in their portrayal of Floyd as a man who left the have-nots alone and robbed only the bankers. What is legendary is the interpretation of his motives. Folklore says that he gave to the poor because of a concern for social justice, but history proves that this was a business proposition: cash paid for protection. But the same could be said of all the other so-called Robin Hood outlaws.

John Ericson as the Oklahoma bank robber in a scene from *Pretty Boy Floyd* (1960).

THE "GOOD" BADMAN IN PROFILE

What distinguishes the "good" outlaw from the "bad" one? First of all, people have to believe that he serves the Higher Law. A Robin Hood is most likely to appear when a certain social situation exists; namely, one in which the law is corrupt. In Anglo-Saxon tradition, "law" and "justice" are assumed to be one and the same. But sometimes the law becomes the tool of a "gang" which must be overthrown, or it comes to represent a system in which injustice is the rule. In such cases, the outlaw, though technically a criminal, may become a folk hero by serving the higher cause of justice. He takes it upon himself, so the legend says, to restore moral order. The audience applauds his crimes because they believe he is motivated by idealism rather than selfishness.

The "bad" outlaw by contrast is seen as lacking such idealism. He has no cause beyond himself. He doesn't give a damn if officials are corrupt, if bankers are cheating poor widows, or if greedy landowners are bullying the tenant farmers. He just wants his share of the pickings, and devil-take-the-hindmost. Thus, interpretation of the motives of individual outlaws determine their place in popular history. The "Robin Hood" robs and (if need be) kills in the interests of the moral law, "for the benefit of society," while the bad badman does so because he's cold-blooded and self-centered.

Hence desperadoes like the Harpe brothers could never belong to the outlaw-hero tradition. Micajah ("Big") Harpe and Wiley ("Little") Harpe preyed on travelers along the Ohio River in 1798-99, gratuitously murdering their victims. "Neither avarice nor want nor any of the usual inducements to the commission of crime, seemed to govern their conduct," wrote Judge James Hall, in 1824. "A savage thirst for blood – a deep-rooted enmity against human nature, could alone be discovered in their actions." Similarly, Clyde Barrow and Bonnie Parker revealed no social purpose in their hit-and-run crimes of the 1930s. "They preyed on their fellow poor," declared Lew Louderback in 1968, "and they killed them when they got in the way."

Second, the good outlaw is identified by his generosity. This trait is demonstrated in the various "steal from the rich and give to the poor" anecdotes. This concept is the keystone in the arch of idealization. Without it, there would be no Robin Hood-type outlaws. When people began to circulate the story that Jesse James had helped a poor widow pay off her mortgage, it was a sign that the outlaw was about to enter the hall of fame. When Woody Guthrie wrote that Pretty Boy Floyd had "sent a Christmas dinner to the families on relief," it indicated that that outlaw was destined for immortality. The outlaw-hero is separated from the more numerous outlaw-villains when enough people believe in his altruism.

Third, the good outlaw must have redeeming personality traits. He's got to be light-hearted, and show some humor now and then. In the ballads, it is usually "jolly Robin" rather than "vicious Robin" or "bloodthirsty Robin." Billy the Kid wins sympathy because he "laughs heartily" during imprisonment (at Las Vegas, New Mexico) while his companions are morose. The idealized badman tells jokes, even if they are of the sardonic variety. When Jesse James, traveling incognito, tells the famous detective that he's in the tomb-stone business, the appreciative audience sees a latter-day Robin Hood.

Furthermore, the badman has got to have some manners; he'll be as courteous as possible. The James Boys "were always polite, deferential, and accommodating" according to Major Edwards. "He had a frank and cordial bearing, which distinguished him and made him beloved by all with whom he came in contact," said John Rollin Ridge of Murrieta. "He had a reputation for being considerate of the old, the young, and the poor; he was loyal to his friends and, above all, loved his mother," said Miguel Otero about Billy the Kid. So there are no Jack the Rippers, rapists, or professional killers among this category of criminals.

Nor will an outlaw ever be called a Robin Hood if he barks at youngsters. Robin Hood is always portrayed as being fond of children, and those who wear his mantle must also meet this requirement. Billy the Kid, reported one woman, asked to hold her baby. When Jesse James stopped at a farmhouse on his way to the Northfield robbery, writes "D.V. Stevens" in *The James Boys in Minnesota* (1882), he "sat playing with a little child" until supper was served.

Fourth, the outlaw hero is seen as the "victim of circumstances." He got bad breaks as a teen-ager and became the target of persecution for one reason or another. Here the Robin Hood tradition reflects the classic question of whether crime is attributable to bad boys or bad environments. The Robin Hood is not innately evil; if only those unfortunate circumstances had not twisted his life out of shape he would have been a successful citizen. He might have become a wealthy rancher, a business executive, even a congressman or a senator! But under extreme provocation he did what any self-respecting man would do, he fought for his rights and thus was "forced" into crime.

The "bad" outlaw, on the other hand, is born morally deformed. The genes went haywire, and the result is a monster in human shape. Indeed, it is the contrast (more apparent in legend than in reality) between the outlaw-leader and some of his gang that highlights this distinction. We are told that Joaquin Murrieta was a prince of a fellow by comparison with the wolfish "Three-Fingered Jack," a degenerate murderer and rapist. Butch Cassidy was a pillar of virture alongside the Sundance Kid and Harvey Logan, both of whom reputedly enjoyed shooting people.

One reason Butch Cassidy must be considered a borderline Robin Hood is because the victim-of-circumstances explanation is not quite convincing in his case. He was not "forced" into crime by persecution, wartime upheavals, or a depression, as were Murrieta, the James brothers, or Charley Floyd. It seems that he was just born to be bad. But, since he was so intelligent and had an engaging personality, some have felt bound to place him among the Robin Hoods anyway. The most common effort to explain his outlawry is to see him an an individualist, caught in a social vacuum created by the disappearance of the open range and the on-rush of an industrial economy. But this has seemed too impersonal an explanation for the popular mind to grasp.

Fifth, the outlaw must be seen as a Trickster. He is intelligent enough to plan successful crimes, and clever enough to escape from his lawman-antagonists. Robin Hood disguised as a potter, butcher, or beggar strolls freely through Nottingham under the very nose of the sheriff. Jesse James is so cagey that − posing as a bumpkin − he joins a posse searching for himself. In Tulsa, Pretty Boy Floyd lives across the street from FBI agents. No outlaw can appeal to the popular fancy unless trickster anecdotes are part of his biography. The trickster is a universal figure in folklore, and the outlaw benefits from this worldwide appeal.

Finally, the Robin Hood has to die in action. He's never captured to spend a life behind bars. That would be too shabby a condition to support the legend. He must die as he lived: violently; in a sharp blast of gunfire. The legend requires that the "good" outlaw, having served his function as a symbol of resistance to oppression, must nevertheless atone for his crimes. Social stability would be imperiled if there were too many outlaws, for then there would be anarchy. So the lesson that "crime does not pay" is either explicitly or implicitly recognized in practically all of the outlaw narratives.

However, the agent of the outlaw's demise, whether lawman or turncoat, has little chance of joining the heroes. Pat Garrett was regarded as a Judas by many (then and now) for shooting Billy the Kid. Captain Harry Love was seen as a mercenary who gunned down innocent Mexicans just to get the reward offered for Joaquin Murrieta. Theoretically, the death of the outlaw should be welcomed by all respectable citizens, no matter how or by whom it was accomplished. But, in fact, there is usually widespread revulsion if the outlaw-chief is betrayed by his own followers. Bob and Charley Ford are the classic examples. They presumably did society a favor by ridding it of a dangerous criminal. But they were scorned in their own lifetimes and have been reviled by many writers ever since as "snakes in the grass." Such are the strange rules by which the game of outlaw hero-worship is played.

The glorification of criminals in print and film distresses many people, including Westerners. Jack Schaefer, for example, denounced the "cult of the badman" in the preface to his *Heroes Without Glory: Some Goodmen of the Old West* (1965). He called for historical writing about those who had done something worthwhile, such as the subjects of his book. Donald Bower, editor of *American West* magazine in 1974, objected to the persistent emphasis on law-breakers in the mass media: "Such glorification of mayhem and idolization of criminals lead inevitably to a depravation of moral standards, and this logically encourages deliberate violation of the tenants [sic] of law and order." Such criticisms have been leveled at outlaws in all times and places, even the great Robin Hood himself. Fourteenth century monks believed he was a bad example, an idol on whom the people should not be wasting their time.

Indeed, everyone has an ambivalent attitude toward the outlaw. On the one hand, nobody seems to think it would be an honor to be shot or robbed by a "Robin Hood." Yet there is a vicarious thrill in seeing or reading about somebody *else's* being robbed or shot at, especially if the victim deserves his come-uppance. This ambivalence is reflected in both the history and the legend of individual outlaws. The varied and often conflicting views about Murrieta, Bonney, Floyd and the others are a prominent part of their biographies.

World history reveals that the idealized outlaw is a universal figure. Every nation at some time has had a brigand whose exploits become the subject of popular legend. Australia's Ned Kelly, Russia's Stenka Razin, Brazil's Lampiao, and Germany's Schinderhannes are examples of the type. They are close to the hearts of the people who endow them with all the virtues of Robin Hood. This idealization reflects the recurrent belief that the bandit may be legally in the wrong, but is morally right.

The "good badmen" possess great appeal because they touch on things that count. Most importantly, they symbolize the age-old dream of individualism. In a world ruled by authority of various kinds, they embody that personal liberty and independence that the bulk of mankind can never enjoy. The price that the actual outlaws pay for their freedom, including constant anxiety and the expectation of violent death, is overlooked in the legend. People view the outlaw's biography selectively, and what they choose to see is a picture of complete freedom.

In addition, people tend to view the outlaw as a social idealist. They want to believe that he cares; that he is a true champion of the underdogs. Human nature gives us ideals, and the outlaw, for many, is the embodiment of such ideals. It is clear that idealization of the outlaw's character and motives leads to the creation of a paragon who never existed. But believing in his generosity and dedication is an act of faith. The cult of the outlaw, like religious belief, is not a subject for practical demonstration.

So the Robin Hoods will continue to live in peoples' memories. For sheer escapism, their biographies are hard to beat. When daily cares seem unbearable, one finds relief in those scenes of long ago, when the bandit rode bold and free. The picture satisfies our longings for a world where there is liberty and justice for everyone.

Bibliography

Chapter 1

THE ROBIN HOOD LEGEND

J. Harris Gable compiled a *Bibliography of Robin Hood* (Lincoln, Neb., 1939) which is rather difficult to use because of its system of organization. The best discussion and text of *The Lytell Geste of Robyn Hode* is in Francis James Child, *The English and Scottish Popular Ballads* (Boston, 1898), III, 40-233. For another detailed analysis, see William R. Clawson, *The Gest of Robin Hood* (Toronto, 1909). Joseph Ritson, *Robin Hood, A Collection of All the Ancient Poems, Songs and Ballads* (London, 1795) is interesting. For general analyses of ballads and broadsides see Evelyn Wells, *The Ballad Tree* (New York, 1950); Leslie Shepard, *The Broadside Ballad* (London, 1962); and David C. Fowler, *A Literary History of the Popular Ballad* (Durham, N.C., 1968). The sketch of Robin Hood by John Major is in a modern printing of the *History of Greater Britain* (Edinburgh, 1892), 156. See also Grafton's *Chronicle* (London, 1809), I,221. The plays of Munday and Chettle are reprinted in Volume 8 of W. Carew Hazlitt (ed.), *A Select Collection of Old English Plays* (London, 1874). The role of ballad figures in the May Games is analyzed in E.K. Chambers, *The Medieval Stage* (Oxford, 1903), I, 174-181.

Thomas Wright's statement is taken from his *Essays on the Literature...of the Middle Ages* (London, 1846), II, 200. An early reference to the fictional connotation of the Robin Hood label is in William Roy's *Rede Me,* originally published in 1525, and reissued by Edward Arber (ed.), in Volume I of *English Reprints* (London, 1869). Joseph Hunter's discussion of the "Wakefield Robin Hood" is in *Critical and Historical Tracts,* no. 4 (London, 1852). The two later books on the same subject are P. Valentine Harris, *The Truth About Robin Hood* (London, 1952), and John William Walker, *The True History of Robin Hood* (Wakefield, 1952), the latter being largely a reprinting of the ballads. The claims for a thirteenth century Robin Hood are advanced in J.C. Holt, "The Origins and Audience of the Ballads of Robin Hood," *Past and Present: A Journal of Scientific History,* no. 18 (November, 1960), 89-110. John M. Gutch in his edition of *A Lytell Geste of Robin Hood* (London, 1847) maintained that the outlaw was a supporter of Simon de Montfort. The best discussion of the history-legend problem is Maurice Keen, *The Outlaws of Medieval Legend* (Toronto, 1961). Also valuable is William Simeone, "The Historic Robin Hood," *Journal of American Folklore*, vol. 66 (October-December, 1953), 303-308.

Chapter 2

ROBIN HOOD CROSSES THE ATLANTIC

Tristram P. Coffin, *The British Traditional Ballad in North America* (Philadelphia, 1963) reprints several Robin Hood ballads. See also William Simeone, "Robin Hood Ballads in America," *Midwest Folklore*, vol. 7 (Winter, 1957), 197-201. For Douglas Fairbanks, consult Ralph Hancock and Letitia Fairbanks, *Douglas Fairbanks: The Fourth Musketeer* (New York, 1953). Ruby Behlmer, "Robin Hood on the Screen," *Films in Review*, vol. XVI (February, 1965), 91-102, discusses the film versions, including the first one produced in 1909.

Michael Martin's confession, published in pamphlet form in 1821, was reprinted as *Captain Lightfoot: The Last of the New England Highwaymen* (Topsfield, Mass., 1926). David Lewis's confession was also published in 1821, and was reprinted by C.D. Rishel as *Life and Adventures of David Lewis, the Robber and Counterfeiter* (Nashville, Penn., 1890). The best discussion of this outlaw is Mac E. Barrick, "Lewis the Robber in Life and Legend," *Pennsylvania Folklife*, vol. 17 (August, 1967), 10-13. A basic tool for the West is Ramon Adams, *Six Guns and Saddle Leather: A Bibliography of Books and Pamphlets on Western Outlaws and Gunmen* (Norman, Okla., 1969).

Chapter 3

JOAQUIN MURRIETA:
A CALIFORNIA ROBIN HOOD?

A good discussion of the background of Mexican outlawry is in Leonard Pitt's *The Decline of the Californios* (Berkeley, 1966).

The Theodore Hittell quotation comes from his *History of California* 4 vols. (San Francisco, 1897), III, 712. For information on Salomon Pico, see J. Gregg Layne, "Annals of Los Angeles," Part II; *California Historical Society Quarterly,* XIII (December, 1934), 327-330; and William H. Ellison (ed.), "Recollections of William A. Streeter, *"C.H.S.Q.* XVIII (September, 1939), 271. The best source for the newspaper stories reporting "Joaquin's" activities is the file at the California State Library in Sacramento, but two commendable efforts at reconstructing the chronology are Remi Nadeau, "Joaquin - Hero, Villain or Myth?" *Westways,* vol. 55 (January, 1963), 18-21, and William B. Secrest, *Joaquin: Bloody Bandit of the Mother Lode* (Fresno, Calif., 1967). The report from the Committee of Military Affairs on the Murrieta reward offer is Document Number 49 of the Assembly, Session of 1853, *Journal of the Assembly,* II. Remi and Margaret Nadeau discuss the identity of the outlaw in "Joaquin: Dead or Alive?", *Westways,* vol. 62 (August, 1970), 45-46; 51. For two near-contemporary views of Joaquin, see the *Tuolumne County Miners and Business Men's Directory* (Columbia, Calif., 1856), and G.F. von Tempsky, *Mitla* (London, 1858), 5-8.

Chapter 4

ROMANTICIZATION OF JOAQUIN

The best discussion of Ridge's background is in Franklin Walker, *San Francisco's Literary Frontier* (New York, 1939), 48-54. See also Joseph Henry Jackson's "Introduction" to the reissue of Ridge's *Life and Adventure of Joaquin Murieta* (Norman, 1955). Ridge's "revenge" statement is printed in Edward Everett Dale and Gaston Litton, *Cherokee Cavaliers* (Norman, 1939), 64; his letter to Stand Watie about the sales of the book is on page 82. The "Joaquin the Horse Thief" song is in *Put's Original California Songster* (San Francisco, 1855), 195. The Michigan variant is discussed in the *Journal of American Folklore,* XXVII (1914), 93. For Ridge's "Third" edition, see Franklin Walker, "Ridge's *Life of Joaquin Murieta:* The First and Revised Editions Compared," *C.H.S.Q.,* XVI (September, 1937), 256-262. The *Police Gazette* story was reprinted by the Grabhorn Press (San Francisco, 1932) with "Notes" by Francis Farquhar, which are a good analysis of the story. This edition has in turn been reprinted (Fresno, 1970) with valuable "supplementary notes" by

Raymund F. Wood and Charles W. Clough. For Hubert Howe Bancroft's "Robin Hood" statement, see volume 34 ("California Pastoral") of his *History of California* (San Francisco, 1888), 642. Hittel's discussion of "Joaquin Murieta and his Banditti" is in *History of California,* II, 712-727. For samples of old-timers' reminiscences, see *History of Tuolumne County* (San Francisco, 1882), 208-216; *History of Solano County* (San Francisco, 1879), 362; and Walter Noble Burns, *The Robin Hood of El Dorado* (New York, 1932), chapter IX. Luis Monguio, "Lust for Riches: A Spanish Nineteenth Century Novel of the Gold Rush and Its Sources," *California Historical Society Quarterly,* 27 (September, 1948), 237-248, describes a novel published at Madrid in 1871, which is based, in part, on the *California Police Gazette* version of 1859. The Owen diary and the Gabutti play are discussed by Raymund F. Wood in "New Light on Joaquin Murrieta," *Pacific Historian,* 14 (Winter, 1970), 54-64. Professor Wood says he has found descendants of Murrieta living in northern Mexico.

Chapter 5

MODERN MURRIETA LEGEND

The Burns citation is in *Columbia Encyclopedia,* 3rd ed., 5 vols. (New York, 1963), III, 1441. Jean-Louis Rieupeyrout, *Le Western* (Paris, 1953), 78-79, discusses the MGM film. J.C. Cunningham edited *The Truth About Murieta* (Los Angeles, 1938). The "Corrido de Joaquin Murieta" is printed in Irwin Silber (ed.), *Songs of the Great American West* (New York, 1967), 135-137. The survey of school children was done by Mrs. Margaret Petteruto at the Washburn School, Los Angeles, on April 11, 1969. Stanford Calderwood's article on "Joaquin Murrieta, Bandit Extraordinary," appeared in *Pacific Pathways,* II (March, 1947), 4-6; 39. For examples of local legends about Murrieta, see Don Juan [John Preston Buschler], *Senor Plummer: The Life and Laughter of an Old Californian* (Hollywood, 1943), 184-188, and Richard Coke Wood, *Tales of Old Calaveras* (Calaveras, 1949), 83. Frank Latta's article, "Sold on Murrieta," is in the *Pony Express,* XXXIV (August, 1962), 3-4. For an interesting analysis of the Gregario Cortes legend, see Americo Paredes, *With His Pistol in His Hand: A Border Ballad and Its Hero*

(Austin, Texas, 1958). Ricardo Montalban's essay on "A Lost Chance" is in the *Hollywood Reporter* "Anniversary Issue," CCVII (November 25, 1969), no page number. For useful insights on movie treatments, see Arthur G. Pettit, *Images of the Mexican American in Fiction and Film* (College Station, Texas, 1980).

Chapter 6

JESSE JAMES: GUERRILLA FIGHTER TO OUTLAW

The most useful source of historical information is William A. Settle, Jr. *Jesse James Was His Name* (Columbia, Mo., 1966). This book is an expanded version of a Ph.D dissertation in history at the University of Missouri, 1945, on "The Development of the Jesse James Legend." Many of the contemporary newspaper reports on the Jameses are on file at the State Historical Society of Missouri in Columbia. Much of the information on Jesse's guerrilla career is in John N. Edwards, *Noted Guerrillas or the Warfare of the Border* (St. Louis, 1877). Also useful is Richard S. Brownlee, *Gray Ghosts of the Confederacy: Guerilla Warfare in the West, 1861-1865* (Baton Rouge, 1958). Henry H. Crittenden [compiler], *The Crittenden Memoirs* (New York, 1936), 340, reprints an interview with Frank James from the Columbia *Herald,* September 24, 1897, in which he credits Jesse with the slaying of Major A.V.E. Johnson. The Heisinger epsiode is recounted in the National Historical Company's *History of Clay and Platte Counties, Missouri* (St. Louis, 1885), 266. Emerson Hough, *The Story of the Outlaw* (New York, 1907), 348, takes an unfavorable view of the brothers. For the Liberty Bank holdup see *James Horan, Desperate Men* (New York, 1949), 39-42 and "Wymore's Plan Restoration of Historic Liberty Bank," *Missouri Historical Review,* LIX (July, 1965), 477-79. The Nathaniel Boswell Manuscript, dictated in 1885, is now in the University of Wyoming Library, Laramie. Boswell says that "in 1878 I arrested Jesse James at Nebraska and put him in jail at Laramie City. When I had him I did not know that it was the noted desperado J.J." Interesting discussions of the amnesty bill of 1875 are in the *Crittenden Memoirs* and in Paul I. Wellman, *A Dynasty of Western Outlaws* (New York, 1961), Chapter III. Stella James, a daughter-in-law of Jesse's, says he wanted to surrender, "Some Notes on Jesse James,"

True West, IX (July, 1962), 28-29. The standard account of the Northfield episode was written by a professor at Carleton College, George Huntington, *Robber and Hero* (Northfield, 1895), and has been reprinted (Minneapolis, 1966). Details of the brother's residence in Tennessee may be found in Settle, *Jesse James Was His Name,* Chapter XII. The Kansas City *Daily Journal* of April 4th devoted two full pages to the James shooting, including the testimony of Mrs. James before the coroner's jury in which she revealed many facts about Jesse's activities. The article was reprinted verbatim as a "special publication" by the Kansas City Westerners in 1950.

Chapter 7

THE MAKING OF A HERO

A useful article on John N. Edwards is Ray Lavery, "The Man Who Made a Folk-God out of Jo Shelby and Created a Legend for Jesse James," Kansas City Westerners *Trail Guide,* VI (December, 1961), 1-15. See also Richard White, "Outlaw Gangs of the Middle Border: American Social Bandits," *Western Historical Quarterly,* XII (October, 1981), 387-408, which sees the James brothers as symbols of masculinity. The William H. Wallace statement is in *Speeches and Writings of William H. Wallace with Autobiography* (Kansas City, 1914), 132. The story of Jesse outwitting the possemen is in Hon. J.A. Dacus, Ph.D, *Illustrated Lives and Adventures of Frank and Jesse James and the Younger Brothers* (St. Louis, 1882), 135. The statement of the James Boys' cruelty to animals is in J.W. Buel, *The Border Bandits* (Philidelphia, n.d.), 4; while Jesse's Corydon speech is in Buel's *The Border Outlaws* (Philadelphia, 1882), 157. Frank Triplett's *The Life, Times and Treacherous Death of Jesse James* (St. Louis and Chicago, 1882), has had a modern reprinting (Chicago, 1970) with an introduction by Joseph W. Snell, who calls it "one of the most pro-James books ever written." Frank James' surrender statement was printed in Horan's *Desperate Men,* 155. Two informative articles on the dime novels are J. Edward Leithead, "The Outlaws Rode Hard in Dime Novel Days," *American Book Collector,* XIX (December, 1968), 13-19, and James I. Deutsch, "Jesse James in Dime Novels; Ambivalence Towards an Outlaw Hero," *Dime Novel*

Roundup, 45 (February, 1976), 13-19. E.C. Perrow, "Songs and Rhymes From the South," *Journal of American Folklore,* XXV (April-June, 1912), 141-149, discusses a collection of Jesse James ballads. John A. and Allan Lomax, *American Ballads and Folk Songs* (New York, 1934), 131, reprints the famous ballad as does Malcolm Laws. *Native American Balladry* (Philadelphia, 1950), 21. H.M. Belden, *Ballads and Songs Collected by the Missouri Folk-Lore Society* (Columbia, Mo., 1955), 401, refers to the Negro convict-author theory. Belden says that the ballad "was sent to me in 1906 by George Williams of Bollinger County, who says 'This song I heard a country boy named Jim Burton sing some eight years ago. Many people in the country know it. I had never seen it in print till lately.'" John O. West, "To Die Like a Man: The 'Good' Outlaw Tradition in the American Southwest," unpub. Ph.D dissertation, Department of English, University of Texas, 1964, includes an appendix with 32 variants of the Jesse James ballad. Regarding the story of Jesse and the Widow Settle in *Jesse James Was His Name,* 227, says that "the earliest published version I am aware of was copied from the Hopkins, Missouri, *Journal* in the Boonville *Weekly Advertiser,* March 19, 1897. "Jesse James, Jr., also told the story in his book, *Jesse James, My Father* (Independence, Mo., 1899), 78-80, placing it in Tennessee. Harry S. Truman's statement is reprinted in Carl W. Breihan's *The Complete and Authentic Life of Jesse James* (New York, 1962), 13. The story of Jesse as Protector of Woman was told by Mrs. Emma Rodge, Le Sueur, Minnesota, and printed in the *Middle Border Bulletin,* VIII (no. 3), 4. Jesse as a kissing bandit is told in Haldeen Braddy, "Jesse James's Chivalry," *Journal of American Folklore,* 69 (January-March, 1956), 66. Homer Croy, *Jesse James Was My Neighbor* recounts the horseshoe legend and the outwitting of "Yankee" Bligh in Chapters 28 and 15, respectively. The Judge Wycoff episode was given to the author by Mrs. Mary G. Harrison of San Jose, California, on August 11, 1969. Clifford Byrne, "Jesse James: Folk Hero," Tennessee *Folklore Society Bulletin,* XX (September, 1954), 47-52, attributes the outlaw's notoriety to the Civil War legacy.

Chapter 8

A TWENTIETH CENTURY LEGEND

The most interesting discussion of the J. Frank Dalton claim is in Homer Croy, *Jesse James Was My Neighbor* (New York, 1949), Chapter 28. See also Phyllis Argall, *The Truth About Jesse James,* (Sullivan, Mo., 1953), which is about Dalton. The Turilli court case is described in an Associated Press dispatch printed in the *Los Angeles Times* of September 30, 1971. Edgar James's "Robin Hood" quotation is from his *Lives and Adventure . . . of the Notorious James Brothers* (Baltimore, 1913), 6. Selections cited in Robertus Love, *The Rise and Fall of Jesse James* (St. Louis, 1926) are on pp. 283, 323, 324. The Palmyra *Spectator* story is reprinted in the *Missouri Historical Review,* XLVIII (July, 1954), 406. Warren Nolan and Owen P. White, "The Bad Man From Missouri," *Collier's* 81 (January 14, 1928), 5; (January 21, 1928), 17-18; (January 28, 1928), 13-14. The Jesse James films are discussed in George N. Fenin and William K. Everson, *The Western: From Silents to Cinerama* (New York, 1962), passim, and in Albert H. Hughes "Jesse James: Outlaw With a Halo," *Montana Magazine of Western History,* XVII (October, 1967), 60-75. John Carradine's reminiscences about *Jesse James* are in Jack Smith's column in the *Los Angeles Times,* November 28, 1971. Jo Frances James's statement appeared among other places in Dixon Wecter, *The Hero in America* (Ann Arbor, Mich., 1963), 352. Short and highly critical views of the James brothers are in Vincent Paul Rennert, *Western Outlaws* (New York, 1968), Chapter Two, and Dorothy M. Johnson, *Western Badmen* (New York, 1970), Chapter Nine. Elizabeth Beall Ginty's *Missouri Legend* has been published in book form (New York, 1938). Allen Case's statement appeared in the *TV Times* section of the *Los Angeles Times,* October 10, 1965. See also Robert Lewis Shayon, "Trigger Happy," *Saturday Review,* XLVIII (October 2, 1965), 31, which discusses the TV series. For an analysis of the movies, see Don Graham, "The Great Northfield Minnesota Raid and the Cinematic Legend of Jesse James," *Journal of Popular Film,* VI (No. 1, 1977), 77-85. Pretty Boy Floyd's letter to the press is reprinted in Lew Louderback's *The Bad Ones* (New York, 1968), 137, while Bonnie Parker's poem is reproduced in Miriam Allen de Ford, *The Real Bonnie and Clyde* (New York, 1968), 136.

Chapter 9

BILLY THE KID: A SHORT AND VIOLENT LIFE

Peter Hurd's statement is in the introduction to Wilbur Coe, *Ranch on the Ruidoso* (New York, 1968), which is also a source for Coe family traditions concerning Billy the Kid. Details about the Kid's childhood were unearthed by Waldo E. Koop, "Billy the Kid, The Trail of a Kansas Legend," Kansas City Westerners *Trail Guide,* 9 (September, 1964), 4-19. See also Robert N. Mullin, *The Boyhood of Billy the Kid* (El Paso, 1957), Monograph #17, in a series of "Southwestern Studies." A number of the early newspaper reports and other documents are reprinted in Peter Hertzog, *Little Known Facts About Billy, the Kid* (Santa Fe, 1964). George W. Coe told what he knew about the Kid in *Frontier Fighter: The Autobiography of George W. Coe* (Boston, 1934). Tunstall's letter and other aspects of his role are discussed in Philip J. Rasch, "Prelude to the Lincoln County War: The Murder of John Henry Tunstall," Los Angeles Westerners *Brand Book,* 7 (1957). Frederick W. Nolan (ed.), *The Life and Death of John Henry Tunstall* (Albuquerque, 1965), 278, says that "concerning the legendary friendship between Tunstall and Billy the Kid, there is no mention of him in the letters, diaries, or any other papers which belonged to J.H. Tunstall." Two of the best histories of the War are by William A. Keleher, *Violence in Lincoln County* (Albuquerque, 1957) and Maurice G. Fulton (ed. Robert N. Mullin), *History of the Lincoln County War* (Tucson, 1968). Taylor Ealy's encounter with the Murphy partisan is described in Ruth Ealy, *Water in a Thirsty Land* (Priv. Printed, 1955), 44-47. An interesting article on the Roberts shooting is Paul Blazer, "The Fight at Blazer's Mill." *Arizona and the West* VI (Autumn, 1964), 203-211. The coroner's verdict in the shooting is reprinted in Keleher, p. 312. Governor Axtell's proclamation is in Fulton, p. 229. A detailed analysis of the fight in Lincoln is in Philip J. Rasch, "Five Days of Battle," Denver Westerners *Brand Book,* XI (1955), 293-323. Rasch also discusses an interesting subject in "The Governor Meets the Kid," *English Westerners Brand Book,* 8 (April, 1966), 5-12. Letters between the Kid and Wallace cited are in Keleher, pp. 211 and 288-89. Details of the Kid's rustling activities are in Charles A. Siringo, *A Texas Cowboy* (Chicago, 1886), 196-199. Many of the contemporary news stories are reprinted in *Billy the Kid: Las Vegas*

Newspaper Accounts of his Career (Waco, Texas, 1958). A thorough description of the Kid's capture at Stinking Springs is in J. Evetts Haley, "Jim East — Trail Hand and Cowboy," *Panhandle-Plains Historical Review,* IV (1931), 39-61. I.M. Bond's recollections about the Kid's trial was printed in the Denver *Post,* February 22, 1903. The theory of the hidden sixshooter was formulated by Leslie Traylor, "Facts Regarding the Escape of Billy the Kid," *Frontier Times,* XIII (July, 1936), 506-513. See also Fulton, p. 394. John W. Poe's "Higher Power" statement occurs in his *The Death of Billy the Kid* (Boston, 1933), 49-50. Details of Garrett's hunt for the Kid are in the well-documented biography by Leon C. Metz, *Pat Garrett: The Story of a Western Lawman* (Norman, 1974).

Chapter 10

A MAN "ALL BAD"

Dime novels about the Kid are listed and briefly discussed in J.C. Dykes, *Billy the Kid: The Bibliography of a Legend* (Albuquerque, 1952). See also Ramon Adams, *A Fitting Death for Billy the Kid* (Norman, 1960), Chapter 2, and Kent L. Steckmesser, *The Western Hero in History and Legend* (Norman, 1965), Chapter VII. Pat F. Garrett's *The Authentic Life of Billy the Kid* has had a modern reprinting (Norman, 1954) with an introduction by J.C. Dykes. Garrett's son, Jarvis P. Garrett, also wrote a lengthy introduction to another edition (Albuquerque, 1964) defending his father's actions. Eve Ball has edited Lily Klasner's *My Girlhood Among Outlaws* (Tucson, 1972), which has much first-hand material on the Lincoln County War and an informative chapter (14) on "Ash Upson: Rolling Stone of the West." For refutations of the story that the Kid stabbed a man in Silver City, see Philip J. Rasch and Robert N. Mullin, "New Light on the Legend of Billy the Kid." *New Mexico Folklore Record,* VII (1952-53), 1-6, and the Jim Blair MS, New Mexico Writers Program, WPA, Santa Fe. Upson's letter to his relative is printed in William A. Keleher, *The Fabulous Frontier* (Santa Fe, 1945), 125. Citations from Siringo, *A Texas Cowboy* (Chicago, 1886) are in Chapter XX-VII, "A True Sketch of Billy the Kid's Life." Examples of Ygenio Salazar's adulatory statements about the Kid may be found in Walter Noble Burns, *The Saga of Billy the Kid* (Garden City, 1926),

Chapter XI, and in Miguel A. Otero, *The Real Billy the Kid* (New York, 1936), 128-129. The verdict of the inquest into the Kid's death is reprinted in Keleher's *Violence in Lincoln County,* 344. The two *corridos* about Bonney are in Aurora Lucero White-Lea, *Literary Folklore of the Hispanic Southwest* (San Antonio, 1953), 139-144. The text of the earliest English-language "Billy the Kid" is printed in John A. Lomax and Alan Lomax, *Cowboy Songs* (New York, 1948), 140. Material cited in Emerson Hough's *Story of the Cowboy* (New York, 1897), 304-316. Arthur Chapman, "Billy the Kid – A Man All 'Bad'." *Outing Magazine,* XLVI (April, 1905), 73-77.

Chapter 11

MR. BONNEY AND THE FAKING OF HISTORY

Harvey Fergusson, "Billy the Kid," *American Mercury* V (May, 1925), 224-231. Citations from Walter Noble Burns, *Saga of Billy the Kid* (Garden City, 1926), are on 69, 67, 140, 184, 52, 228, 176, 129. Lily Klasner, *My Girlhood Among Outlaws,* Chapter 21 on "Bob Olinger As I Knew Him." For the ballad, see D.K. Wilgus, "The Individual song: Billy the Kid," *Western Folklore,* XXX (July, 1971), 226-234. Moses Asch (ed.) *American Folksong, Woody Guthrie* (New York, 1961), 29, prints a version of the ballad. *New Mexico: A Guide to the Colorful State* (New York, 1940), 104. C.L. Sonnichsen and William V. Morrison, *Alias Billy the Kid* (Albuquerque, 1955) examines the Brushy Bill Roberts case. Frank G. Applegate, "New Mexico Legends," *Southwest Review,* XVII (Winter, 1932), 201-208. Statements cited in Miguel Otero, *The Real Billy the Kid* (New York, 1936) are on pp. 178, 129, and 167. Mrs. Sophie Poe's statement was recorded by Fred Mazzula and W.T. Moyers in 1950, and is included in *The Badmen,* Columbia Records LL-1013 (issued in 1963). Text of Copland's ballet is printed in Rosalyn Krakova, *New Borzoi Book of Ballet* (New York, 1956), 42-46. For comments on the Billy the Kid films, see George N. Fenin and William K. Everson, *The Western: From Silents to Cinerama* (New York, 1962), 36, 242, 266, and Frank Mancel, *Cameras West* (Englewood Cliffs, N.J., 1971), 90-94. "Billy the Kid: In two Films About Him Hollywood Fakes History," *Life,* August 4, 1941, 65-69. Edwin Corle, *Billy the Kid* (New York, 1953); Charles Neider, *The Authentic Death of Hendry Jones* (New York, 1956); Amelia Bean, *Time for Outrage* (Garden City, 1967). Statements from Frazier Hunt, *The Tragic Days of Billy the Kid* (New York, 1956), are on 74, 302, 108, 303. William Lee Hamlin, *The True Story of Billy the Kid* (Caldwell, Idaho, 1959), 200. For films, Fenin and Everson, *The Western,* p. 340. Frank Price's view of the Kid was expressed in Cecil Smith's column of the *Los Angeles Times,* February 23, 1972. Interesting comments on the film *Chisum* are in Jenni Calder, *There Must Be a Lone Ranger: the American West in Fact and in Film,* (New York, 1975), 210-212. See also Stephen Tatum, *Inventing Billy the Kid: Visions of the Outlaw in America, 1881-1981* (Albuquerque, 1982), a sophisticated study of how interpretations of the Kid change with social and cultural circumstances. The university professor was Howard R. Lamar, "Political Patterns in New Mexico and Utah Territories, 1850-1900," *Utah Historical Quarterly,* 28 (October, 1960), 364. George Curry, *An Autobiography* (Albuquerque, 1958) 44. Ealy, *Water in a Thirsty Land,* p. 26.

Chapter 12

THE DUBIOUS ROBIN HOOD: BUTCH CASSIDY

Parker's birthplace is given in Lula Barker Betenson and Dora Flack, *Butch Cassidy, My Brother* (Provo, Utah, 1975), 32. Details of the Telluride robbery are in Charles Kelly, *The Outlaw Trail: A History of Butch Cassidy and His Wild Bunch,* rev. ed. (New York, 1959), 29-31. Pearl Baker, *The Wild Bunch at Robbers Roost* (New York, 1971) is good on local history and has a chapter (16) on Cassidy. Some details of Cassidy's career in the early 90s are revealed by one of his friends, Matt Warner, *Last of the Bandit Riders* (Caldwell, Idaho, 1940). Bob Calverly's letter about his arrest of Cassidy, originally published in the *Wyoming State Journal,* June 16, 1939, is reprinted in Larry Pointer, *In Search of Butch Cassidy* (Norman, 1977), 72-73. See also Betenson, 96-98.

Accounts of the formation of the Wild Bunch are in Kelly, 128-130, and in James D. Horan, *Desperate Men* (New York, 1949), 208 ff. For a well-photographed retracing of the hideouts and escape routes, see Robert Redford, *The Outlaw Trail* (New York, 1978). Mrs. Betenson's statement about the Castle Gate robbery is on page 126. For the most astute analysis of the outlaws' probable movements in South America, see Pointer, Chapters 18 and 19. For variants of the Poor Widow story, see Betenson, 130-131; Kelly 154-155; and Pointer, 103-104. Arthur Chapman, "Butch Cassidy," *Elks Magazine* (April, 1930). Kelly's "generosity" statement occurs on page 209. For the controversy in Utah after Kelly's book came out, see the review of his second edition by William M. Purdy in *Utah Historical Quarterly*, XXVIII (January, 1960), 80-81. For a sample of the regional interest in Cassidy, see Wallace Stegner, *Mormon Country* (New York, 1942), 284-291. Statements about the success of the film are in Will Wright, *Six Guns and Society: A Structural Study of the Western* (Berkeley, 1975), 95 and Lloyd Shearer, "The Return of Butch and Sundance," *Parade,* (May 28, 1978), 9-10. Edward Lipton's review was in *Film Daily,* September 10, 1969, 6. William Goldman's statements are in the printed screenplay, *Butch Cassidy and the Sundance Kid* (New York, 1975), preface and 52. For examples of the "Robin Hood" publicity following the motion picture release, see Charles Hillinger, "Butch Cassidy's Sister Tells of His Deeds," *Los Angeles Times,* April 3, 1970. The anecdote about Price, Utah, is reported in Betenson, page 126.

Chapter 13

END OF TRAIL: PRETTY BOY FLOYD

The most important source of information is Vivian Brown, "The Real Story of Pretty Boy," a six-part series of newspaper articles published in the *Oklahoma News,* October 24-October 30, 1934. W.R. Draper's pamphlet *On the Trail of "Pretty Boy" Floyd* (Girard, Kansas, 1946) is also useful. Draper was a reporter for the Kansas City *Journal Post* and a correspondent for the United Press, and he spent much time in the Cookson Hills. Chapter Two of Myron Quimby, *The Devil's Emissaries* (New York, 1969), entitled "Phantom of the Ozarks," has material on Floyd's early arrest record. Lew Louderback, *The Bad Ones* (New York, 1968) has an exceptionally well-researched chapter on the outlaw, including a convincing refutation of the Kansas City Massacre charge. On this affair, see also Blackie Audett, *Rap Sheet* (New York, 1954), Chapter Two. Paul I. Wellman, *A Dynasty of Western Outlaws* (New York, 1961) has a chapter on Floyd which contains some inaccuracies. See Don Congdon (ed.), *The Thirties* (New York, 1961), 217, for background on law enforcement problems. Jay Robert Nash, *Citizen Hoover* (Chicago, 1972) is critical of Hoover's record in the Thirties. The Adair County ballad of "Pretty Boy Floyd" was sung in December 1962, by Dean Joe J. Keen of the University of Colorado Summer School, and is printed in the Colorado Folksong Bulletin, vol. 2 (1963), 103. The text of Guthrie's "Pretty Boy Floyd" is in John Greenway, *American Folksongs of Protest* (Philadelphia, 1953), 296-297 along with a discussion of the singer's role in folk music history.

For the controversy over the FBI's role, see the editorial "Questions for the FBI," *Los Angeles Times*, October 28, 1974; letters from Clarence M. Kelley and Clyde Ware, *Los Angeles Times*, November 23, 1974; and "FBI Executed Outlaw, Ex-Officer Says," *Los Angeles Times*, October 27, 1979.

Chapter 14

THE "GOOD" BADMAN IN PROFILE

Mody G. Boatright, "The Western Bad Man as Hero," *Publications of the Texas Folklore Society*, XXVII (Dallas, 1975), 96-105, is a classic analysis. Judge Hall's statement about the Harpes is quoted in Otto A. Rothert, *The Outlaws of Cave-in-Rock* (Cleveland, 1924), 57. Lew Louderback's comment about Bonnie and Clyde is in *The Bad Ones* (New York, 1968), 76. *The James Boys in Minnesota* is discussed in Horst H. Kruse, "Myth in the Making: The James Brothers, the Bank robbery at Northfield, Minn., and the Dime Novel," *Journal of Popular Culture*, X (Fall, 1976), 315-326. Emmett Dalton with Jack Jungmeyer, *When the Daltons Rode* (New York, 1931) has interesting observations on the inconsistent attitude of the American public toward malefactors, especially in Chapter XXIII ("Kissing the Rogue"). Orrin Klapp, "The Clever Hero," *Journal of American Folklore*, 67 (January-March, 1954), 21-34, discusses several outlaws as "tricksters." Ramon Adams, *Six Guns and Saddle Leather*, rev. ed. (Norman, 1969) is a comprehensive bibliography which notes historical and folkloric aspects of books on Western outlaws. See also his *Burs Under the Saddle: A Second Look at Books and Histories of the West* (Norman, 1964). Donald E. Bower, "The

Robin Hood Myth," *American West*, XI (July, 1974), 48. For general overviews of the outlaws, see Eric Hobsbawm, *Bandits* (New York, 1969), which looks at them from a Marxist position. Kent L. Steckmesser, "Robin Hood and the American Outlaw," *Journal of American Folklore*, 79 (April-June, 1966), 348-355. Lloyd J. Wood, "The Robin Hood Motif: Outlaws as Literary Heroes," unpub. M.A. thesis, Department of English, University of Hawaii, 1971. Richard Dorson, *American Folklore* (Chicago, 1959), 236-245, and Richard E. Meyer, "The Outlaw: A Distinctive American Folktype," *Journal of the Folklore Institute*, XVII (May-December, 1980), 94-124.